Cultural Tools for
Interpreting the Good News

John J. Pilch

THE LITURGICAL PRESS
Collegeville, Minnesota

www.litpress.org

Cover design by David Manahan, O.S.B. Illustration courtesy of Flat Earth Photos.

Nihil obstat: Robert C. Harren, *Censor deputatus.*
Imprimatur: ✠ John F. Kinney, Bishop of St. Cloud, Minnesota, April 8, 2002.

1   2   3   4   5   6   7   8

Library of Congress Cataloging-in-Publication Data

Pilch, John J.
    Cultural tools for interpreting the Good News / John J. Pilch.
        p. cm.
    Includes bibliographical references.
    ISBN 0-8146-2826-5 (alk. paper)
        1. Bible N.T. Gospels–Social scientific criticism. 2. Sociology, Biblical. 3. Jews–Social life and customs–To 70 A.D. 4. Palestine–Social life and customs–To 70 A.D. I. Title.

BS2555.6.S55 P55 2002
226'.067–dc21   2002072975

In loving memory of
Jean Peters Pilch
(1936–1997)
proud daughter of the Diocese of Little Rock
resting in the peace of God at
Calvary Cemetery
Fort Smith, Arkansas

Contents

Introduction

The challenge of reading the Bible and interpreting it respectfully and correctly is similar to the challenge of serving on a jury and reaching the correct verdict. An article published in *Psychological Science* in 1994 reported the results of a research project investigating "how well do jurors reason?" The researchers selected 154 subjects across the age span from fifteen through sixty, across the educational span from ninth grade to some college course work, and across economic diversity. They listened to a twenty-five-minute audiotape reenactment of the *Commonwealth of Massachusetts v. Frank Johnson* murder trial.

The undisputed events in this case were that Frank Johnson and Alan Caldwell (who had a razor) met in a bar early one day, argued, and Caldwell threatened Johnson with the razor. That evening Johnson returned to the bar, then went outside with Caldwell, and they both got into a fight. Johnson knifed Caldwell to death. The disputed elements were: Did Caldwell pull the razor? (It was found in the back pocket of his corpse.) Did Johnson actively stab Caldwell or stick the knife out to protect himself? How did they get outside together? Did Johnson go home deliberately to get his knife? Why did Johnson return to the bar?

From this evidence, jurors were charged to construct a plausible narrative structure or story or scenario of what happened. Then they were given a set of verdict alternatives:

1

murder 1, premeditated and with malice; murder 2, malice; manslaughter, some guilt; self-defense, no guilt. They were also given the criteria associated with each verdict. Their challenge was to find an acceptable match between the scenario they had constructed and the appropriate verdict categories.

The researchers discovered, as expected, that many jurors created *multiple scenarios* from the incomplete evidence that was open to conflicting interpretations. They sought to construct a scenario that would utilize the most consistent and least discrepant evidence. These jurors felt confident and certain of the scenario they created and its accompanying verdict, but honestly admitted that other scenarios for interpreting the evidence were also possible. In other words, they could imagine different verdicts.

A surprising number of jurors constructed a single scenario, often very early during the process. Then they disregarded any evidence that didn't fit that scenario and retained the evidence that did. Such jurors had absolute certainty about their scenario and the appropriate verdict and could not imagine any other plausible scenario.

Reading and interpreting the Bible requires that the reader imagine scenarios for the books and passages being read. But the Bible is also a high-context document. This means that the authors of the Bible safely assumed that they did not have to present their audiences or readers with all the details of the stories and events they were reporting. For example, the evangelist John simply notes that it was noon when a woman of Samaria came to Jacob's well to draw water (John 4:6-7). A modern Western reader would imagine this to be public space, hence there is nothing wrong with this picture. This same reader is puzzled to learn that when his disciples returned to the scene, they "were amazed that he was talking with a woman" (John 4:27). Western readers see nothing wrong with that, either.

The evangelist, however, was writing for his contemporaries. He rightly presumes that his audience or readers immediately realize that everything is wrong with this picture. Why clutter the story with unnecessary details? The woman is in the wrong place at the wrong time. Modern readers in

Western culture should be very grateful to the Yahwist for telling us an important piece of cultural information about women and wells. Abraham's servant in search of the proper bride for Isaac made his camels kneel down outside the city of Nahor by the well of water at the time of evening, "the time when women go out to draw water" (Gen 24:11). With this information, we can now appreciate that without having to be explicit, the evangelist John presents the Samaritan woman as not being an honorable woman, as having no sense of shame. She should not be at the well at this hour. Nor should either of them be talking to the other in this place and time. All the worse if they are there alone. Thus, a modern Western reader who is accustomed to creating a "Western cultural scenario" for reading about Jesus and the Samaritan woman in John must be prepared to replace that with a more plausible, first-century Mediterranean reading scenario. The interpretation of the story will be different.

Indeed the appropriate Mediterranean interpretation may well leave the modern Western reader with a new challenge. How can reading the Bible in its appropriate Mediterranean cultural context shed light on concerns of believers who live in Western or other cultures? It isn't simply the two-thousand-year gap that poses problems. It is the fact that people from other cultures are reading a Mediterranean document and often seek in it "all the direct answers for living" (American Catholic Bishops' Statement on Fundamentalism, 1987). American Catholic Bishops wisely cautioned against this because the Bible nowhere makes such a claim.

In its 1994 document *Interpreting the Bible in the Church,* the Pontifical Biblical Commission reminded Bible readers that the task of interpretation involved three steps which can be summarized in this way. First, one must know one's culture very well. Second, one must know the Bible's culture well. Third, one must then begin to build a bridge between the two cultures. In this book we will focus mainly on understanding the Mediterranean cultural world in which our ancestors in the faith lived and in which the Bible originated. The principal task will be to provide a Western reader with basic Mediterranean cultural concepts with which to create appropriate scenarios for imagining what one is reading. The hope is that believers will thus be equipped to understand what the sacred authors wrote and what they meant. These cultural concepts will help believers learn "the honest truth about Jesus" (Second Vatican Council Dogmatic Constitution on Divine Revelation, #19), the Mediterranean man. Only then will it be possible to begin to appropriate the Bible for personal or community life.

Feast of St. Hedwig of Silesia and St. Margaret Mary

John J. Pilch

October 16, 2001

Georgetown University and the University of Pretoria, South Africa

Chapter One

Honor and Shame

Every culture is guided by core values, powerful forces that drive people's behavior. Instrumental activism is the core value in the United States reflected chiefly in its conviction that technology will provide the solution to all problems. The driving force in people's lives is to actively master and be in control of the environment: nature, time, space, other individuals, and even other societies. This core value is further replicated in specific values like democracy, which facilitates individual instrumental mastery. This would include free enterprise, equal opportunity, individualism, pragmatism, future orientation—everything that helps a citizen to make it in mainstream society. In a word, all these values drive human behavior and social interaction in mainstream U.S. society.

The core value of our ancestors in the faith (members of the house of Israel, see Matt 10:6) is interpersonal contentment. This value directs people to accept human finitude and limitations, but still to seek to have a genuine human existence that is also free. This is replicated in honor and shame. Honor is the public claim to worth and the public acknowledgment of that claim. Shame is the public denial of that claim. When the father publicly commands his son to work in the vineyard, for example, he is making a public claim to honor. The son who replied affirmatively (even though he did not go) publicly honored the father. The son who publicly refused (even though he ultimately went) publicly shamed the father (Matt 21:28-30). Notice that Jesus did not ask about honor in that story, but about doing the father's will.

Shame can also be positive, that is, a person is sensitive to his or her honor and does what has to be done in order to protect and enhance it. Negative shame is exhibited by a person who has no regard for maintaining honor and observing the honor code. Let us examine some passages in detail to understand how these values direct and control the behavior of our ancestors in the faith.

Positive Shame

Joseph Learns that Mary Is Pregnant

> Now this is how the birth of Jesus Christ came about. When his mother Mary was betrothed to Joseph, but before they lived together, she was found with child through the holy Spirit. Joseph her husband, since he was a righteous man, yet unwilling to expose her to shame, decided to divorce her quietly. Such was his intention when, behold, the angel of the Lord appeared to him in a dream and said, "Joseph, son of David, do not be afraid to take Mary your wife into your home. For it is through the holy Spirit that this child has been conceived in her. She will bear a son and you are to name him Jesus, because he will save his people from their sins." All this took place to fulfill what the Lord had said through the prophet:
> "Behold, the virgin shall be with child and bear a son,
>   and they shall name him Emmanuel,"
> which means "God is with us." When Joseph awoke, he did as the angel of the Lord had commanded him and took his wife into his home. He had no relations with her until she bore a son, and he named him Jesus (Matt 1:18-25).

The topic sentence (v. 18) is confusing in translation, isn't it? The passage does not actually speak about the birth of Jesus until the last verse! The Greek word in verse 18, *genesis,* would be better translated along the lines of: "These are the circumstances surrounding or connected with the conception of Jesus." It is important to distinguish betrothal from engagement. The ancient world did not know of engagement, a process in which two self-selected partners agree to consider marriage at some not too distant time. Marriage was the union of two families, or better, the fusion of the honor of two families. It was arranged, generally by the mothers, and publicly ratified in the village by the fathers. Parents were viewed to be acting in the name of God (Matt 19:6) The ideal marriage partners were patrilateral cousins; that is, a son would marry his father's brother's daughter (see Gen 24:4, 15, 24, 47). But the mothers could rearrange the choices (see Gen 29:21-27). The bride and groom were not considered as individuals but rather as representatives of their families. Jesus' prohibition against divorce (Matt 19:6) is rooted in the realization that divorce would initiate a feud between the families that could escalate to violence and perhaps result in bloodshed. Blood feuds would last for generations, hence it was best to avoid them.

Betrothal initiated the contract, and moving into the husband's house after the wedding completed it. Sons, single and married, will always live with their father in a large compound (perhaps even an entire village). Prior to Mary moving in with Joseph, "she was found with child." The passive voice means others found out. How? If Mary is already beginning to show, she is far advanced in the pregnancy. But given the kinds of robes women wore, how would others see that Mary is beginning to show?

Perhaps a better clue is in the prescription God gave concerning women and their menstrual flow (see Lev 15:19-33). A woman is considered unclean at this time and must isolate herself from contact with others. Afterward she must make a sacrifice of atonement before the Lord for her unclean flow. In later tradition, which might not have existed yet in the first century, a woman had to take a ritual bath. These baths, like the village ovens, were communal. While Mary might have tried to hide the fact, the normally busybody women of the village would have learned it and spread the news. Joseph may well have been the last to find out!

Realizing how shocking this story might be to his readers, Matthew inserts a reassuring comment to the report: Mary was pregnant through a holy spirit (the Greek lacks a definite article here and in v. 20). Our ancestors in the faith did not have a concept of impersonal causality. Hebrew has no expression like "it rained." Rather, God sent the rain. Some person is always responsible. If no human person can be identified, then it must be an other-than-human person, namely, a spirit. In this instance, Matthew tells the readers it was a holy (rather than a capricious or malicious) spirit. If one remembers what the spirit did for Samson (read Judg 13:24; 14:6, 19; 16:20), one can readily appreciate the role of the spirit in Matthew's report. The spirit empowered him to kill a lion bare-handed and to kill thirty men single-handedly. Spirit always means power.

Since Matthew describes Joseph as a righteous man, the reader immediately knows the predicament in which Joseph finds himself. The Israelites recognized two kinds of righteous or "holy men." A *ṣaddiq* was an ordinary person who did his best to observe the law of God. A *ḥasid* was so concerned with pleasing God that he went beyond the basic. If it was necessary to wash one's hands before eating in order to please God, the *ṣaddiq* might be satisfied with washing the palms, but the *ḥasid* might wash up to and beyond the elbow just to be sure (see Mark 7:1-5).

At the very least, Joseph knows the child is not his. If he were to accept that child he would be a thief, which would displease God. Further, he knows that since Mary is already pregnant, he and she will not be able to produce a blood-speckled sheet to show to the wedding guests as custom required when they consummate their marriage (see Deut 22:13-29). He doesn't want to get that far in the process, because it would be shameful for both of them ("unwilling to expose her to shame"). In addition, the righteous Joseph knows that he can submit Mary, as a suspected adulteress, to trial by ordeal (read Num 5:11-31). This, too, he is willing to forego ("decided to divorce her quietly" or better, "leniently").

How do Mediterranean people solve problems? Very often the solution will come in a dream. Dreams or other such experiences in the Bible give a person new information, help a person select a new direction in life, give affirmation. In a dream Joseph learns that Mary's pregnancy is God's doing; he also learns the gender of the child and the name to give him. When Joseph wakes up (v. 24), he follows the insights received in the dream.

Negative Shame

Between the end of Joseph's dream and the moment he wakes up, Matthew inserts the well-known citation from Isaiah 7:14. To understand this high context excerpt from Isaiah, we need first to read this selection from 2 Kings 16. Isaiah knew this background and could reasonably expect that his readers knew it too.

Background for Understanding Matthew's Use of Isaiah 7

In the seventeenth year of Pekah, son of Remaliah, Ahaz, son of Jotham, king of Judah, began to reign. Ahaz was twenty years old when he became king, and he reigned sixteen years in Jerusalem. He did not please the LORD, his God, like his forefather David, but conducted himself like the kings of Israel, and even immolated his son by fire, in accordance with the abominable practice of the nations whom the LORD had cleared out of the way of the Israelites. Further, he sacrificed and burned incense on the high places, on hills, and under every leafy tree.

Then Rezin, king of Aram, and Pekah, son of Remaliah, king of Israel, came up to Jerusalem to attack it. Although they besieged Ahaz, they were unable to conquer him. At the same time the king of Edom recovered Elath for Edom, driving the Judeans out of it. The Edomites then entered Elath, which they have occupied until the present.

Meanwhile, Ahaz sent messengers to Tiglath-pileser, king of Assyria, with the plea: "I am your servant and your son. Come up and rescue me from the clutches of the king of Aram and the king of Israel, who are attacking me." Ahaz took the silver and gold that were in the temple of the LORD and in the palace treasuries and sent them as a present to the king of Assyria, who listened to him and moved against

Damascus, which he captured. He deported its inhabitants to Kir and put Rezin to death.

King Ahaz went to Damascus to meet Tiglath-pileser, king of Assyria. When he saw the altar in Damascus, King Ahaz sent to Uriah the priest a model of the altar and a detailed design of its construction. Uriah the priest built an altar according to the plans which King Ahaz sent him from Damascus, and had it completed by the time the king returned home. On his arrival from Damascus, the king inspected this altar, then went up to it and offered sacrifice on it, burning his holocaust and cereal-offering, pouring out his libation, and sprinkling the blood of his peace-offerings on the altar. The bronze altar that stood before the LORD he brought from the front of the temple—that is, from the space between the new altar and the temple of the LORD—and set it on the north side of his altar. "Upon the large altar," King Ahaz commanded Uriah the priest, "burn the morning holocaust and the evening cereal-offering, the royal holocaust and cereal-offering, as well as the holocausts, cereal-offerings, and libations of the people. You must also sprinkle on it all the blood of holocausts and sacrifices. But the old bronze altar shall be mine for consultation." Uriah the priest did just as King Ahaz had commanded. King Ahaz detached the frames from the bases and removed the lavers from them; he also took down the bronze sea from the bronze oxen that supported it, and set it on a stone pavement. In deference to the king of Assyria he removed from the temple of the LORD the emplacement which had been built in the temple for a throne, and the outer entrance for the king. The rest of the acts of Ahaz are recorded in the book of the chronicles of the kings of Judah. Ahaz rested with his ancestors and was buried with them in the City of David. His son Hezekiah succeeded him as king (2 Kgs 16:1-20).

The event reported is taking place in the year 734/733 B.C.E. Pekah, king of Israel (the Northern Kingdom) and Rezin, king of Syria, form an alliance to attack and conquer Jerusalem. They intended to replace Ahaz, king of Judah, with a non-Davidic puppet king. In fear (Isa 7:2), Ahaz sacrifices his son in the valley of Hinnom just outside Jerusalem in order to appease God's wrath (2 Kgs 16:3). The Israel-Syrian attempt was unsuccessful, but Ahaz realized that other attempts might indeed succeed. His choices were to risk defeat by the invaders or to seek help from a stronger nation. He chose the latter course and courted Assyrian help. Notice the high price at which this help comes, and the king's infidelity to his own faith traditions. The author of 2 Kings paints a very shameful picture of a shameless Davidic king. As he is inspecting Jerusalem's water supply, Ahaz comes face to face with Isaiah accompanied by his young son, Shear-yashub, whose name means "A remnant shall return."

Isaiah's Oracle for King Ahaz

In the days of Ahaz, king of Judah, son of Jotham, son of Uzziah, Rezin, king of Aram, and Pekah, king of Israel, son of Remaliah, went up to attack Jerusalem, but they were not able to conquer it. When word came to the house of David that Aram was encamped in Ephraim, the heart of the king and heart of the people trembled, as the trees of the forest tremble in the wind.

Then the LORD said to Isaiah: Go out to meet Ahaz, you and your son Shear-jashub, at the end of the conduit of the upper pool, on the highway of the fuller's field, and say to him: Take care you remain tranquil and do not fear; let not your courage fail before these two stumps of smoldering brands [the blazing anger of Rezin and the Arameans, and of the son of Remaliah], because of the mischief that Aram [Ephraim and the son of Remaliah] plots against you, saying, "Let us go up and tear Judah asunder, make it our own by force, and appoint the son of Tabeel king there."

Thus says the LORD:
This shall not stand, it shall not be!
Damascus is the capital of Aram,
and Rezin the head of Damascus;
Samaria is the capital of Ephraim,
and Remaliah's son the head of Samaria.
But within sixty years and five,
Ephraim shall be crushed, no longer a nation.
Unless your faith is firm
you shall not be firm!

Again the LORD spoke to Ahaz: Ask for a sign from the LORD, your God; let it be deep deep as the nether world, or high as the sky! But Ahaz answered, "I will not ask! I will not

tempt the LORD!" Then he said: Listen, O house of David! Is
it not enough for you to weary men, must you also weary my
God!? Therefore the Lord himself will give you this sign: the
virgin shall be with child, and bear a son, and shall name him
Immanuel. He shall be living on curds and honey by the time
he learns to reject the bad and choose the good. For before
the child learns to reject the bad and choose the good, the
land of those two kings whom you dread shall be deserted.

The LORD shall bring upon you and your people and your
father's house days worse than any since Ephraim seceded
from Judah. [This means the king of Assyria.] On that day

The LORD shall whistle
  for the fly that is in the farthest streams of Egypt,
  and for the bee in the land of Assyria.
All of them shall come and settle
  in the steep ravines and in the rocky clefts,
  on all thorn bushes and in all pastures.

On that day the LORD shall shave with the razor hired from
across the River [with the king of Assyria] the head, and the
hair between the legs. It shall also shave off the beard (Isa
7:1-20).

The name of Isaiah's son is part of Isaiah's message. But
as with many sayings of the prophets, the name Shear-
jashub is rife with ambiguity. The Hebrew can indeed be
read as reported: "A remnant will return." The meaning of return is turn to God, repent (see Isa 6:10). A negative reading
would say: "Disaster will indeed come, and *only* a remnant
shall return or repent." A positive view would see a promise
in that name: "A remnant *will indeed* return or repent."

Isaiah assures Ahaz that the nations he presently fears
will eventually pose no threat at all (vv. 4-9). Isaiah con-
cludes this part of his message with a pun on the Hebrew
word for faith or belief, here translated as "firm" (see v. 9).
Forget, indeed cancel your political alliances, and rely exclusively on God who will be loyal to the covenant made with
David and David's descendants which includes Ahaz!

Isaiah gave Ahaz one more chance when the king began
to sketch out political strategies with other trusted advisers.
The prophet urged the king to seek a sign from the Lord. This

is not a miracle or some extraordinary event. The sign is rather some event that confirms a prophet's word, and Israelites were capable of understanding it because they had a vivid sense of God's role in human experience and human events. The prophet often pointed to the sign or performed one.

Ahaz responds to the prophet's invitation with feigned piety ("I will not tempt the LORD!"), since he intends to stick with his alliance with Assyria. Isaiah then identifies the sign that would confirm his word of doom for the Israel-Syria alliance against Jerusalem and his word of grace for the Davidic dynasty. The sign is the birth of a child whose name will point to his significance: God is with us. "Behold, a young woman of marriageable and child bearing age is already pregnant [or will soon be pregnant] and is about to give birth to a son. She shall name him Immanuel."

Like all prophets, Isaiah announces the will of God for here and now. His message is for Ahaz, and it may well be that his wife is already pregnant and will give birth to a son to replace the son/heir to the throne whom he had killed. Isaiah was not looking into a distant future for two reasons. First, peasants have no concept of future, but are forced by circumstances of life to focus intensely on survival in the present. Also, the Hebrew language of the Bible does not have a future tense or other tenses familiar to us. The action of a verb is either complete or incomplete. Something incomplete awaits completion, and in the peasant understanding, this would have to be soon in order to be meaningful.

By the time this youngster reached maturity, the alliance between Syria and Israel against Jerusalem would be ended, and the Lord will have "shaved" Judah with an Assyrian razor (Isa 7:15-24). The disaster that Assyria will bring will be far worse than that threatened by Syria and Israel.

Thus, when Matthew inserts Isaiah 7:14 into his report of how Joseph deals with the pregnancy of his wife, Mary, the evangelist is reinterpreting Isaiah for his purposes. That is of course how Catholic tradition has understood Matthew's report and his use of Isaiah. Yet, even with the citation from Isaiah, the entirety of Matthew's report still rings with shock and shame to readers who are sensitive to the values of honor and shame. Mediterranean readers would immediately recognize this. To prepare such readers for this shock, Matthew cleverly begins his story of Jesus with a genealogy.

Ascribed Honor

The Lineage Record of Jesus Messiah

The book of the genealogy of Jesus Christ, the son of David, the son of Abraham.

Abraham became the father of Isaac, Isaac the father of Jacob, Jacob the father of Judah and his brothers. Judah became the father of Perez and Zerah, whose mother was Tamar. Perez became the father of Hezron, Hezron the father of Ram, Ram the father of Amminadab. Amminadab became the father of Nahshon, Nahshon the father of Salmon, Salmon the father of Boaz, whose mother was Rahab. Boaz became the father of Obed, whose mother was Ruth. Obed became the father of Jesse, Jesse the father of David the king.

David became the father of Solomon, whose mother had been the wife of Uriah. Solomon became the father of Rehoboam, Rehoboam the father of Abijah, Abijah the father of Asaph. Asaph became the father of Jehoshaphat, Jehoshaphat the father of Joram, Joram the father of Uzziah. Uzziah became the father of Jotham, Jotham the father of Ahaz, Ahaz the father of Hezekiah. Hezekiah became the father of Manasseh, Manasseh the father of Amos, Amos the father of Josiah. Josiah became the father of Jechoniah and his brothers at the time of the Babylonian exile.

After the Babylonian exile, Jechoniah became the father of Shealtiel, Shealtiel the father of Zerubbabel, Zerubbabel the father of Abiud. Abiud became the father of Eliakim, Eliakim the father of Azor, Azor the father of Zadok. Zadok became the father of Achim, Achim the father of Eliud, Eliud the father of Eleazar. Eleazar became the father of Matthan, Matthan the father of Jacob, Jacob the father of Joseph, the husband of Mary. Of her was born Jesus who is called the Messiah.

Thus the total number of generations from Abraham to David is fourteen generations; from David to the Babylonian exile, fourteen generations; from the Babylonian exile to the Messiah, fourteen generations (Matt 1:1-17).

Genealogies in antiquity were drawn up only after a person died and became famous! The same was true of childhood. No one remembered it, but after a person died and became famous, a "stereotypical" childhood was drawn up. Jesus died a shameful death; crucifixion was reserved for the worst criminals. But shortly after his death, Jesus was seen alive again by his friends. Since only God can raise someone from death, and God wouldn't do this for a shameful person, the raising of Jesus from death by God bestowed unimaginable honor upon Jesus. His life story would therefore require that all this honor be spelled out in detail.

The purpose of the genealogy is not primarily factual information but rather a deliberate attempt to connect a person to a family group in the present which has roots in the past and to give some inkling of what one might expect of this person. The genealogy also communicates honor, primarily ascribed honor. Ascribed honor is the reputation that one inherits at birth, but it can also be ascribed by God, the king, or elites. This means honor can be ascribed by those who can claim honor for others and force public acknowledgment of that honor because they have the power and standing to do so.

Matthew has artificially given Jesus three sets of fourteen generations because he wants to link Jesus closely with David. The Hebrew form of David is DVD, and each successive consonant of the Hebrew alphabet is used as a number. Thus, $D = 4$ and $V = 6$: $DVD = 4 + 6 + 4 = 14$. David's name in Hebrew adds up to fourteen. For Matthew, David is a key element of Jesus' ascribed honor: he can trace lineage back to King David, the source of Jesus' family honor.

But David does not stand at the head of the genealogy; he is not the apical ancestor. The ancestor at the head of the list (apex = head, hence apical) is the one in the light of whom all others are to be interpreted or reinterpreted. Abraham, the first patriarch, heads Matthew's listing of the genealogy of Jesus. He is the one who received the divine promises of children, land, and reputation. But since David is mentioned next at the head of the list, Matthew intends that the reader interpret "son of Abraham" in terms of "son of David." Abraham now takes on royal significance. The Greek translation of the Hebrew Bible, the Septuagint, renders Genesis 23:6 this way: "You [say the Hittites to Abraham] are a king from God among us." Thus, Matthew seems to be familiar with the Israelite tradition which associated Abraham with kingship and incorporates it into Jesus' genealogy by associating Abraham with David.

This is precisely the problem Jesus faces in the rest of the gospel story line. Judean leaders reject Jesus' kingship (Matt 21:15-16; 27:42). Matthew promotes Jesus' claim to Judean royal lineage in his list of Jesus' ancestors. Moreover, the story of Jesus' birth which follows the genealogy indicates divine parentage by a miraculous birth. In the literature of Mediterranean antiquity "dual paternity" was an established way of expressing miraculous birth, kingly authority, and divine power. For example, Augustus was reputed to be the son of Octavius *and* the god Apollo (Sallust, *Lives of the Caesars* 2.94.1-7). Thus kin groups provided one form of legitimation: the presence of Joseph in the lineage established Jesus' political right to the throne of David and/or social status. Divine procreation provided another legitimation: this will be a great leader since he has divinely ascribed honor.

Acquired Honor

What about the women in this lineage? (Tamar 1:3; Rahab 1:5a; Ruth 1:5b; Bathsheba 1:6, and Mary.) They testify to Jesus' honor as it was acquired by them as pivotal, exogamously related women in the lineage. (Exogamous is a technical term in family studies describing marriage between partners who are not members of the same family, in this case, not patrilateral cousins, the customary marriage partner in ancient Israel.)

Tamar was Judah's daughter-in-law who had to trick him into providing her children when he failed to assign one of his sons to give her dead husband an heir. Judah pronounced that "she is more in the right than I am" (Gen 38:26), or "Tamar acted more honorably than I did." Thus did Tamar acquire honor for herself.

Rahab (1:5a) protected Israelite spies in Jericho, her own city! The Israelites paid back their debt by sparing her entire kin-group and including her into Israel (Josh 6:25).

Ruth (1:5b) was a foreigner (a Moabite) from the land of one of Israel's ancient enemies, yet she acted loyally to Naomi and Naomi's kin group. She received a new husband, Boaz, from Naomi's kin group, and a son, Obed (Ruth 4:13-22). Ruth acted with honor to the benefit of an Israelite family.

The context of Bathsheba's relationship to David is basically shameful. David acquired her through adultery, conspiracy, and murder (2 Sam 11:1–12:35). But she bore Solomon (Jedidiah, "Yah's beloved," 2 Sam 12:24-25) and promoted Solomon over Adonijah as next king (1 Kgs 1:11-21, 28-31; 2:13-25). Solomon bowed down to her and provided her with huge honor: a throne at his right hand (1 Kgs 2:19).

Finally, Mary acquired honor because she was obedient to the divine will and gave birth to Jesus (Matt 1:16) as a virgin (1:18, 23, 25). Thus Mary's shame of pregnancy before marriage is turned into honor in the birth account that follows the lineage. All these women showed initiative, that is, they acquired honor. The biblical stories about Tamar, Rahab, and Ruth state this explicitly by means of formal declarations and blessings. Concerning Bathsheba and Mary, the acquired honor is implied. In summary, Jesus' ascribed honor according to Matthew not only derives from his paternal lineage but also from the acquired honor of key, exogamously related women in the lineage.

Acquiring Honor by Challenge and Riposte

A Mediterranean person is born into an honor rating which must be protected and defended through all of life. This is ascribed honor. It can never be augmented, but it can be besmirched. Acquired honor, on the other hand, can, of course, be acquired or gained. A very common, everyday way of gaining honor is to play the game known technically as "challenge and riposte," but can be translated as "push and shove." Riposte is a fencing term describing a sharp, swift thrust that one makes after parrying an opponent's lunge. In ordinary language, it is a quick, witty, sarcastic, cutting, but very appropriate and devastating retort. In the Mediterranean world, every question is a challenge. No question is considered harmless. The suspicion is that the questioner is trying to embarrass someone into admitting he does not know the answer to the question. Of course, no one will ever admit this, so the questioner will always receive an answer but without any assurance it is correct and trustworthy. The life-game of challenge and riposte can only be played by equals. In this next text segment, we see that Jesus is in the region of Tyre and Sidon, a geographical designation pointing to southern Phoenician territory. He is approached by a Canaanite woman seeking a favor. The woman is not his equal on three counts: by gender, by origin (Canaanite), and by residence. She is ineligible to play the game of challenge and riposte.

Jesus, Master of Insult

> Then Jesus went from that place and withdrew to the region of Tyre and Sidon. And behold, a Canaanite woman of that district came and called out, "Have pity on me, Lord, Son of David! My daughter is tormented by a demon." But he did not say a word in answer to her. His disciples came and asked him, "Send her away, for she keeps calling out after us." He said in reply, "I was sent only to the lost sheep of the house of Israel." But the woman came and did him homage, saying, "Lord, help me." He said in reply, "It is not right to take the food of the children and throw it to the dogs." She said, "Please, Lord, for even the dogs eat the scraps that fall from the table of their masters." Then Jesus said to her in reply, "O woman, great is your faith! Let it be done for you as you wish." And her daughter was healed from that hour (Matt 15:21-28).

The woman's request is respectfully phrased even if yelled out. The Greek word describes a shout implying an unpleasant nature of the sound; the tense indicates it was of some duration. We would call this a nuisance or say she was "making a scene." It is, of course, typically Mediterranean since all public behavior is considered a "scene." She requests pity from Jesus. In Mediterranean culture, to have pity means to pay one's debts, to meet one's interpersonal obligations (recall "interpersonal contentment" as a core Mediterranean value). She need say no more than this to get her message across.

She also addresses Jesus very respectfully as "Lord" (equivalent to Sir, Mister), but adds "Son of David." Comparison with Mark (7:24-30) indicates that Matthew probably added this to the story. This tallies well with the point of Matthew's lineage report. He deliberately continues to portray Jesus as legitimate heir to the throne of David, a king. Here, a complete foreigner recognizes this status. Then she presents her request: "My daughter is tormented by a demon."

Jesus' reply is perfect for the culture. He ignores her (v. 23). She is not his equal, he is not obliged to respond to her request. The disciples call his attention to the obvious: she is making a scene! Dismiss her, or chase her away. To them but within her earshot, Jesus repeats his single-minded dedication to exclusive ministry to "the lost sheep of the house of Israel." Matthew's Jesus is a true-to-form Mediterranean male in this encounter. He is unswervingly faithful to his in-group.

The woman presses her case still further. She is behaving very shamefully. She should neither approach nor speak to an unrelated male in public. But what does she have to lose? She is not of his in-group, she is not his equal. All he can do is ignore or reject her. He has already ignored her. She now approaches and does homage. This means she has prostrated herself at his feet, blocking his progress. He will have to jump over her, walk around her, or kick her out of the way. She begs straightforwardly: Lord (respectfully once again), help me, give me what I need, what I should have, what is necessary. Her daughter's condition makes it impossible to arrange a marriage for the daughter. That means the family will remain weak relative to other families, since marriage is the fusion of two families. Her daughter's condition also makes her unreliable for doing chores for the family. This is a serious loss to the family.

Jesus replies *as he usually does* to questioners: with an insult. (Jesus is the master of insult: in Luke 10:25 he asks a lawyer about his reading ability; in Matt 5:21, 27, 33, 38, 43 he asks illiterate peasants what they heard. Jesus' favorite insult is for the Pharisees, whom he calls hypocrites [actors] in Matt 6:2, 5, 16; 7:5; 15:7; 22:18; 23:13, 17 [compare his prohibition of using this word in Matt 5:22], 23, 25, 27, 29; 24:51, and the coup de grace, questioning their paternity in Matt 23:33.) Jesus uses a "dog" word in his response to her. To use a "dog" word relative to a woman is not nice in any language. Many a woman in this situation would flee the scene as quickly as possible. She is losing, and the crowd is watching to see the end result and to determine who should be declared the winner in this push and shove contest. The woman doesn't flee at all. She comes back with a clever and appropriate riposte: even dogs get to eat in their master's household. The unnamed woman has won the contest. It is the only one Jesus loses until his trial and death.

Good loser that he is, Jesus' response might be translated: "Touché, woman! You can give as good as you get. Favor granted!" A closer look at the verse, however, reveals two key culturally significant ideas. One, it is the woman's loyalty (faith) that has gained a favorable response from Jesus. Faith in Mediterranean culture is best translated "loyalty," or "I'm sticking with you no matter what!" This indeed the woman did while being ignored and then insulted by Jesus. Two, the passive voice points to God as the healer. "Let it be done for you [by God, of course!], as you wish" and "her daughter was healed [by God, of course] from that hour." Jesus is God's broker, the one who puts needy clients in contact with the patron, the one who can do for people what equals cannot.

Chapter Two

How a Mediterranean Boy Becomes a Man

Even though the customary marriage partner in the Ancient Middle East and the Bible is a patrilateral cousin, the woman is not fully welcome or accepted into the groom's family. She never really fits in; she is always suspect. After all, she is the daughter of another family and her loyalties understandably remain divided if not entirely rooted in her family of origin. Matters will remain this way until she bears a son. A son will be "social security" for the mother. The closest emotional bond in this culture exists between mother and eldest son. In Western culture, we might describe this relationship as "co-dependent" personality. In the circum-Mediterranean world including Middle Eastern culture, this relationship is quite normal. Readers might be familiar with adult males in some circum-Mediterranean cultures who continue to live at home to a late age (by American standards) putting off marriage for as long as possible. And after marriage, there is a never-ending tug toward mother and home. If you have grasped the importance for a woman to bear a son in this culture, what do you imagine the barren Hannah screamed in reply to the questions of her husband, Elkanah: "Hannah, why do you weep, and why do you refuse to eat? Why do you grieve? Am I not more to you than ten sons?" (1 Sam 1:8).

The newborn son is raised exclusively by the women (mother, sisters, and other females in the family compound) with no male role model until adolescence (puberty). In this rigidly gender-divided culture, the young boy under the age of puberty lives in the women's quarters with all the women and girls and is pampered and pleasured. He is breast fed twice as long as the girls. "Son," said the mother of the seventh of her sons who faced death, "have pity on me, who carried you in my womb for nine months, *nursed you for three years,* brought you up, educated and supported you to your present age" (2 Macc 7:27), emphasis added. Mothers who read this story remark that a three-year-old has teeth! But a three-year-old can also speak. When he says: "Feed me!" he is fed without hesitation. It takes no stretch of imagination to conclude that a boy raised in this fashion would find little difficulty in writing the creation story as it is reported by the Priestly author in Genesis 1. God simply says: "Let there be . . ." and it happens. All boys know from experience that all they have to do is say: "Feed me," and they get fed. Every boy's word is effective!

At the age of puberty the boy is unceremoniously pushed out of the comfortable women's world into the harsh male world. There is no rite of passage. Bar mitzvah did not exist until Talmudic times (around 500 C.E.) The boy continues to run back to the women's world, but is returned time and again to the men's world until he realizes he must stay there.

The Boy Jesus in the Temple

> Each year his parents went to Jerusalem for the feast of Passover, and when he was twelve years old, they went up according to festival custom. After they had completed its days, as they were returning, the boy Jesus remained behind in Jerusalem, but his parents did not know it. Thinking that he was in the caravan, they journeyed for a day and looked for him among their relatives and acquaintances, but not finding him, they returned to Jerusalem to look for him. After three days they found him in the temple, sitting in the midst of the teachers, listening to them and asking them questions, and all who heard him were astounded at his understanding and his answers. When his parents saw him, they were astonished,

and his mother said to him, "Son, why have you done this to us? Your father and I have been looking for you with great anxiety." And he said to them, "Why were you looking for me? Did you not know that I must be in my Father's house?" But they did not understand what he said to them. He went down with them and came to Nazareth, and was obedient to them; and his mother kept all these things in her heart. And Jesus advanced [in] wisdom and age and favor before God and man (Luke 2:41-52).

At the age of twelve Jesus should have already moved from the world of the women into the world of the men. He should already have begun learning from Joseph and other male kin how to behave like an adult male. Luke tells us (v. 43) that Jesus "remained behind in Jerusalem, but his parents did not know it." This would raise a red flag for all Mediterranean readers. Either Mary and the woman's group with whom Jesus would have been associated, or Joseph and the men's group, should have known his whereabouts. In the Mediterranean world, one does not separate from the group and wander off alone. Especially not a twelve-year-old boy.

Notice, however, that it takes a day's journey in the caravan before Joseph and Mary discover that he is not there. Imagine the scenario. Travel alone, even as a family, is dangerous. Caravan is the customary mode of travel. Like all space in the ancient Middle-Eastern world, caravans are divided along gender lines. All the woman and girls and boys younger than the age of puberty travel as a group. All the men and boys older than the age of puberty travel as a group. Imagine Mary boasting among the women: "Do you see my son, Jesus? Is he here with us women? Of course not! He is now a man! He is with the men! I'm so proud of him." Then imagine Joseph with his head hung low in the men's segment. Others are asking him: "Where is your twelve-year-old son, Jesus? Why isn't he here?" And Joseph thinking to himself: "I'm embarrassed! That twelve-year-old is still with the women. What a disappointment. It's time he began to act like a male, it's time for him to become a man. Oh, I'm so ashamed!"

It isn't until the end of the first day of a four- or five-day journey back to Nazareth that Joseph and Mary discover that Jesus is nowhere in the caravan: neither among relatives nor acquaintances. Since travel in general is deviant, the safest and most comfortable manner of travel is with relatives and friends who would form the caravan. Think, in passing, who these relatives might be: grandmother(s) and grandfather(s), uncles and aunts, cousins. Acquaintances, just like the relatives, would certainly be from Nazareth where the family lived. In general, people outside of Nazareth would be suspect. The irresponsible boy Jesus has caused a huge problem for Joseph and Mary. They must join another caravan with strangers for the trip back to Jerusalem. Presumably two caravans traveling in opposite directions met when they stopped. If not, the return trip could be delayed! To travel alone would be suicide. Then they spend three days searching for Jesus in Jerusalem. Imagine how two devout, observant members of the House of Israel would react to such behavior of a son.

The first-century walled city of Jerusalem was densely populated, with the estimated population of the entire country at about 250,000. Jerusalem might have had about 10,000 inhabitants. It was considered one of the two (maybe three) "real" cities at that time. Festivals would swell the population, but then only 10 percent of the city's population lived in the city. The rest lived in the environs, and this is where visitors would be, too. That Joseph and Mary could find Jesus after a three-day search is rather extraordinary. Quite likely the last place where they would expect to find him would be the Temple.

That scenario is perhaps the most interesting. He is sitting among teachers, listening and asking questions that amaze the listeners because of his understanding and his answers. Where indeed did this son of an artisan gain such wisdom? That question is difficult to answer, but more important than that answer is the fact that with this behavior Jesus manifests that he has successfully negotiated the transition from boyhood into the adult male world. If Joseph was disappointed in Jesus during the first day of the caravan trip to Nazareth, he is very proud at this moment. Luke repeats this reaction (amazement; astonishment by others) to Jesus more than once in his Gospel (Luke 4:32; 5:9; 8:56), thus indicating that Jesus is gaining honor. On each of these occasions people recognize that Jesus is much more than one might conclude on the basis of his background as an artisan's son from a small hamlet (his ascribed honor).

Sitting in the midst of teachers indicates Jesus is a learner in this setting, he is not a teacher. But he is obviously a capable learner for he listens carefully and asks relevant questions concerning Torah. The audience is also impressed not only by his questions but also by his penetrating answers to the teachers' questions. While Joseph and Mary are at first happy to find him, Mary's question reflects a curious lack of understanding (given what she learned about Jesus in chapter one of Luke) and a mild rebuke. Remembering the strong, life-long emotional bond that exists between mother and son, it is easy to understand the pain Jesus has caused Mary—and Joseph too!—by his irresponsible and shamefully disobedient behavior. Because they had to leave the caravan, Joseph and Mary were put in a very awkward, indeed dangerous, predicament.

Jesus' reply to both of them (you plural) also carries a note of reproach. Did Joseph not care enough about him to keep a closer eye on him? It is shameful if a father is unable to control his family. Perhaps the best interpretation of Jesus' statement in addition to the mild reproach is that he is becoming aware of a special relationship to God as his heavenly Father, and his earthly parents ought to have perceived and understood this.

The reproachful tone of Jesus' question directed to Mary indicates not only that he is talking down to her but also that he is perhaps beginning to think about establishing a fictive kinship group, a surrogate family. Joseph would be pleased to see that Jesus is beginning to distance himself from customary Mediterranean maternal claims on him. This is part of how one becomes a man in this world. Surrogate family and the high price of giving up one's biological family are a favorite theme for Luke (9:57-62; 12:51-53; 14:26; 18:28-30).

In the end, Jesus returns to Nazareth with Joseph and Mary and continues to obey them even as he grows to manhood. "Keeping all these things in her heart" means Mary resumed her Mediterranean maternal role of monitoring what is happening in her family. Luke's final comment emphasizes that Jesus' honor, reputation, maturity, and stature continue to grow not only among fellow human beings but also in the eyes of God. Jesus is on the way to becoming an honorable male and obedient son in his culture.

Raising a Dutiful Son

> He who loves his son chastises him often,
>> that he may be his joy when he grows up.
> He who disciplines his son will benefit from him,
>> and boast of him among his intimates.
> He who educates his son makes his enemy jealous,
>> and shows his delight in him among his friends.
> At the father's death, he will seem not dead,
>> since he leaves after him one like himself,
> Whom he looks upon through life with joy,
>> and even in death, without regret:
> The avenger he leaves against his foes,
>> and the one to repay his friends with kindness.
>
> He who spoils his son will have wounds to bandage,
>> and will quake inwardly at every outcry.
> A colt untamed turns out stubborn;
>> a son left to himself grows up unruly.
> Pamper your child and he will be a terror for you,
>> indulge him and he will bring you grief.
> Share not in his frivolity lest you share in his sorrow,
>> when finally your teeth are clenched in remorse.
> Give him not his own way in his youth,
>> and close not your eyes to his follies.
> Bend him to the yoke when he is young,
>> thrash his sides while he is still small,
> Lest he become stubborn, disobey you,
>> and leave you disconsolate.
> Discipline your son, make heavy his yoke,
>> lest his folly humiliate you (Sir 30:1-13).

The family, usually rather large and quite extended, is the central social institution in Middle Eastern culture. It must be strong enough to hold its own against other families who are always considered to be enemies to one's own family. For this reason, the patriarch (father) must be able to impose his will on his sons and must be able to count on loyalty from them. The more sons he has, the more powerful will be the father (see Ps 127:3-5). Because boys are brought up by the women and pampered, the father's task is to teach the boy how to be a man when the youngster enters the male world at the age of puberty.

Since there was no rite of passage in ancient Israel, the young boy was unceremoniously pushed by the women into the harsh and hierarchical men's world. Understandably, the youngster ran back to the comfort of the women's world where he was treated much better. But that was no longer to be. Physical discipline was the major strategy by which men taught young boys how to be men. A Mediterranean man was and is expected to suffer unspeakable pain without flinching or screaming. He must learn how to suffer in silence. The book of Proverbs advises fathers more than once to physically discipline their sons.

> Withhold not chastisement from a boy;
>> if you beat him with the rod, he will not die.
> Beat him with the rod,
>> and you will save him from the nether world (Prov 23:13-14; see also 13:24; 19:18; 22:15; 29:15, 17).

Sirach frames his poem with that same advice: chastise the son often (30:1), beat his ribs (30:12), discipline him and make heavy his yoke (30:13).

The chief result of raising a son in this manner is that the boy brings great honor to his father. Notice that the father will boast of him to his friends. Such a father dies with no regrets, for not only has he left behind someone like himself, a "chip off the old block," but his son will be an "avenger" (v. 6). The Hebrew word literally means "next of kin," but can also be translated as "avenger" and "redeemer." The avenger is that son in the family who will take revenge in order to sustain the family's honor, even if he mistakenly kills the wrong person (Num 35:9-15). The avenger plays a very important role in the family (Lev 25:25).

Failure to raise a son properly will bring sad results which Sirach spells out in verses 7-13. In his parables, Jesus presented some examples. The father of the so-called prodigal son does not seem to have raised his sons appropriately (Luke 15:11-21). The younger son's request is equivalent to wishing his father were dead. The father failed to extract loyalty from him. For a while the elder son in the story appears to be loyal. He reveals his own true colors, however, when the father receives the wayward son with a feast. Instead of rejoicing, the elder son scolds the father and slanders his brother. In another of Jesus' parables, the man who asks each of his two sons to work in his vineyard succeeded in teaching one about honor (the one who answered "yes") but he clearly was less successful in imposing his will upon him. The other son behaved shamefully toward his father, but ultimately did honor the father by doing his will (Matt 21:28-32). In this story, notice that Jesus does not ask who behaved honorably, but rather who actually obeyed the father.

A Truly Obedient Son

Some time after these events, God put Abraham to the test. He called to him, "Abraham!" "Ready!" he replied. Then God said: "Take your son Isaac, your only one, whom you love, and go to the land of Moriah. There you shall offer him up as a holocaust on a height that I will point out to you." Early the next morning Abraham saddled his donkey, took with him his son Isaac, and two of his servants as well, and with the wood that he had cut for the holocaust, set out for the place of which God had told him.

On the third day Abraham got sight of the place from afar. Then he said to his servants: "Both of you stay here with the donkey, while the boy and I go on over yonder. We will worship and then come back to you." Thereupon Abraham took the wood for the holocaust and laid it on his son Isaac's shoulders, while he himself carried the fire and the knife. As the two walked on together, Isaac spoke to his father Abraham: "Father!" he said. "Yes, son," he replied. Isaac continued, "Here are the fire and the wood, but where is the sheep for the holocaust?" "Son," Abraham answered, "God himself will provide the sheep for the holocaust." Then the two continued going forward.

When they came to the place of which God had told him, Abraham built an altar there and arranged the wood on it. Next he tied up his son Isaac, and put him on top of the wood on the altar. Then he reached out and took the knife to slaughter his son. But the LORD's messenger called to him from heaven, "Abraham, Abraham!" "Yes, Lord," he answered. "Do not lay your hand on the boy," said the messenger. "Do not do the least thing to him. I know now how devoted you are to God, since you did not withhold from me your own beloved son." As Abraham looked about, he spied a ram caught by its horns in the thicket. So he went and took the ram and offered it up as a holocaust in place of his son. Abraham named the site Yahweh-yireh; hence people now say, "On the mountain the LORD will see."

Again the LORD's messenger called to Abraham from heaven and said: "I swear by myself, declares the LORD, that because you acted as you did in not withholding from me your beloved son, I will bless you abundantly and make your des-cendants as countless as the stars of the sky and the sands of the seashore; your descendants shall take possession of the gates of their enemies, and in your descendants all the nations of the earth shall find blessing—all this because you obeyed my command."

Abraham then returned to his servants, and they set out together for Beer-sheba, where Abraham made his home (Gen 22:1-19).

On the basis of the principles for raising sons presented in this chapter thus far, it seems clear that Abraham had done a fine job raising Isaac. Since the lad was old enough to carry the wood, he was also old enough to run for his life when the situation began to dawn on him with clarity. He doesn't flee at all but even permits his father to tie him up and place him atop the wood on the altar. There is no indication that he is crying, screaming, resisting. That would be shameful behavior. He resolved to go to his death honorably. Isaac remains an obedient son even in the face of death. In submitting to Abraham's will, Isaac shows he is honorable, just as his father acts honorably in submitting to God's will. God intervenes, and Abraham sacrifices a ram instead of his only, beloved son.

Nearly two thousand years later, the Second Book of Maccabees recounts two similar reports of males accepting death with honor rather than disgracing themselves and their fathers by seeking to escape. These reports reflect the period of the Syrian King Antiochus Epiphanes, who attempted to replace Judaism and its system of worship with paganism and worship of pagan gods in the Temple at Jerusalem. Eleazar, a very honorable ninety-year-old scribe, was being forced to eat pork (2 Macc 6). He spit it out and so was sentenced to death. Some already paganized friends advised him to pretend to eat and thus escape the death penalty. He chided them for suggesting he should betray God' s laws and prove disloyal to God whom he had served faithfully since his childhood. Moreover, he refused to give a bad example to younger men who looked on. Throughout this chapter, a wide array of honor vocabulary relative to Eleazar's behavior is repeated. Eleazar, a *foremost* scribe, of *noble appearance*, preferred a *glorious death* to a life of defilement. He had *courage* to reject the unlawful food. He made his mind up in a *noble manner, worthy* of his years, the *dignity* of his advanced years, and the *admirable life* he had lived from childhood. Can the reader continue to identify the other honor vocabulary in this passage? Eleazar's choice of death with honor rather than continued life in disgrace is praised.

In the very next chapter (2 Macc 7), the sacred author reports the story of seven brothers murdered in sequence (after gruesome torture) from oldest to youngest in the presence of their mother for refusing to eat pork and prove disloyal to God. "Filled with a noble spirit that stirred her womanly heart with *manly courage*" (an interesting point!), she [the unnamed mother of these sons] exhorted each of them in the language of their forefathers to face death bravely since God will eventually raise them (2 Macc 7:21-23). The persecutors hoped to use the last son to bend the mother's will. Pretending to encourage her youngest to eat the pork, she instead encouraged him to be worthy of his brothers. She died after he died.

Eleazar and seven sons who preferred death with honor are examples of cultural heroes, that is, the kind of honorable adult male every young man should aspire to grow up to be. To be fully prepared for this eventuality, fathers physically disciplined their sons so that they would learn how to suffer in silence even to the point of death if necessary.

Paul, a Cultural Hero

> Are they ministers of Christ? (I am talking like an insane person.) I am still more, with far greater labors, far more imprisonments, far worse beatings, and numerous brushes with death. Five times at the hands of the Jews I received forty lashes minus one. Three times I was beaten with rods, once I was stoned, three times I was shipwrecked, I passed a night and a day on the deep; on frequent journeys, in dangers from rivers, dangers from robbers, dangers from my own race, dangers from Gentiles, dangers in the city, dangers in the wilderness, dangers at sea, dangers among false brothers; in toil and hardship, through many sleepless nights, through hunger and thirst, through frequent fastings, through cold and exposure. And apart from these things, there is the daily pressure upon me of my anxiety for all the churches. Who is weak, and I am not weak? Who is led to sin, and I am not indignant? (2 Cor 11:23-29).

Since approximately only 2 percent of the population were literate, Paul's letters were read to an assembled audience. It is plausible to imagine this audience as interactive, that is, interjecting or commenting as the spirit moved them. To a Western reader, this passage sounds like the statement of a masochist. In the Mediterranean world, response would be quite different. By presenting a catalogue of his sufferings, Paul presents himself as a hero in his culture. The heroic way in which he accepted and survived these afflictions is similar to the way in which Isaiah's Servant responds to mistreatment and suffering (Isa 42:1-4; 49:1-7; 50:4-11; 52:13–53:12). Paul has not only experienced suffering, but he apparently also has experience in relating his sufferings. The first list, including labors, imprisonments, beatings, and near death, is presented in ascending order of danger. One can imagine the listening audience gasping as the list progresses. Perhaps they even begin to make sounds of admiration and approval ("oooh," "ah!"). Forty lashes minus one is punishment with mercy, that is, making sure that the punishment would not be exceeded in case of a miscount (Deut 25:2-3). Punishment with rods was often inflicted by a Roman magistrate (see Acts 16:22). The stoning may have taken place at Lystra (Acts 14:5, 19).

The journeys Paul undertook to spread the gospel also entailed danger and suffering, especially if he traveled alone (that is, without kin or companions, as appears to have been the case) rather than in a caravan or something of that sort. As Paul, like all Mediterranean males, learned how to suffer in the physical discipline received from his father, so Paul in the service of God reasons analogously that he will demonstrate his loyalty by pressing forward in evangelization even though it involves extensive suffering. In this text-segment, it is clear that Paul is not unique. He reports this catalogue because other ministers have claimed honor in this manner, too. Paul seeks to assert a greater claim to honor than his opponents.

Jesus' Death with Manly Honor

It was nine o'clock in the morning when they crucified him. The inscription of the charge against him read, "The King of the Jews." With him they crucified two revolutionaries, one on his right and one on his left. [This verse, "And the scripture was fulfilled that says, 'And he was counted among the wicked,'" is omitted in the earliest and best manuscripts.] Those passing by reviled him, shaking their heads and saying, "Aha! You who would destroy the temple and rebuild it in three days, save yourself by coming down from the cross." Likewise the chief priests, with the scribes, mocked him among themselves and said, "He saved others; he cannot save himself. Let the Messiah, the King of Israel, come down now from the cross that we may see and believe." Those who were crucified with him also kept abusing him.

At noon darkness came over the whole land until three in the afternoon. And at three o'clock Jesus cried out in a loud voice, *"Eloi, Eloi, lema sabachthani?"* which is translated, "My God, my God, why have you forsaken me?" Some of the bystanders who heard it said, "Look, he is calling Elijah." One of them ran, soaked a sponge with wine, put it on a reed, and gave it to him to drink, saying, "Wait, let us see if Elijah comes to take him down." Jesus gave a loud cry and breathed his last. The veil of the sanctuary was torn in two from top to bottom. When the centurion who stood facing him saw how he breathed his last he said, "Truly this man was the Son of God!" (Mark 15:25-39).

Mark's report of the death of Jesus presents him as a perfect Mediterranean male behaving in the most honorable way as he faces death. Very early in the gospel story line, Jesus has made enemies of powerful people (Pharisees and Herodians) who resolve to kill him (Mark 3:6). His family takes immediate action to save his life: they declare him crazy ("He is out of his mind," Mark 3:21). In the ancient Israelite world, if someone shamed another and did not make appropriate amends, that other person or his "avenger" (see above) was obliged to kill him. There is no escaping this fate, except if the family declared the offending member "crazy." But now the "crazy" family member cannot leave the family circle, nor can he marry. All "normal" life comes to a halt. The offender might as well be dead. Jesus, however, does not pull back or practice greater caution. He continues until the chief priests and scribes find a way to arrest him and have him put to death (Mark 14:1-2).

When Jesus is put on trial (Sanhedrin, Mark 14:53-65; Pilate, Mark 15:1-15), the game of challenge and riposte, of competing for honor, is over. Going to court is shameful. A person who feels compelled to take another to court admits defeat by that course of action, even though that person may have bribed the judge(s) to win the case (see Matt 5:25-26: the only way out of jail is to bribe one's way out). The community knows grievances should be worked out apart from the courts since they were so unreliable (Prov 25:8-10). Even Jesus affirmed that wisdom (Matt 5:25). Now that Jesus finds himself "in court," as it were, there is no way he can win. He did not have the wherewithal to head this off. In these final days, of the twelve Jesus handpicked, one betrayed him, one denied him, and all abandoned him. So his best strategy now is to suffer in true manly fashion with cryptic responses or in silence.

Notice that Jesus is crucified at nine A.M. Passersby revile him. The chief priests and scribes challenge him. Those crucified with him also abused him verbally. At noon darkness came over the land until three P.M. Jesus has hung on the cross for six hours, and in Mark's account he hasn't spoken or cursed or cried or shouted . . . or even boasted! At three P.M., Jesus cries something out in Aramaic. While our written text is quite clear to read, and Mark provides a translation, the bystanders were obviously confused. They thought he was calling Elijah.

Research on crucifixion notes that victims of crucifixion did not die from loss of blood but rather from suffocation. The posture of the crucified person makes it impossible for the diaphragm to work properly. The lungs do not inflate sufficiently with oxygen, and one gradually suffocates. Suffocation is not a pleasant sight to witness. Some cancers destroy the lungs making breathing difficult and eventually impossible. The person's mouth is open to grasp more oxygen. It becomes dry, and speech is unintelligible if not entirely impossible. What Jesus said after six hours on the cross was quite likely so garbled, it was misunderstood. Shortly after that, he shrieked and died.

The response of the centurion reported by Mark is very significant: "Truly this man was the Son of God" (Mark 15:39). The Greek text does not have a definite article before son, hence the proper translation of the centurion's remark is "a son of god." Since the centurion was not a believer but rather a pagan, we must consider what "a son of god" would mean to a person like him. As a soldier in charge of "one hundred" men (actually eighty) who were not always engaged in battle, he was familiar with how stalwart soldiers amused themselves. They would have contests of strength, and often one man was stronger than all. Such a soldier would be considered more than human, better than human, or "a son of god," that is, having god-like qualities. The centurion's comment recognizes something about Jesus that is extraordinary.

Specifically what impressed the centurion is "how he breathed his last," that is, the manner in which he died. Perhaps this centurion witnessed many crucifixions. The victim was naked, stress caused him to befoul himself, the experience made the victim nearly crazy. He would scream, curse, shriek, cry. Few if any crucified people died like Eleazar, the seven young men, or like Jesus! In effect, the centurion says: "I have seen many men crucified, but I have never seen anyone die like this: bearing his pain and suffering in silence and screaming only at the very end! Truly extraordinary. God-like!"

This interpretation is a culturally plausible explanation of the event as it may indeed have occurred at the actual crucifixion. In Mark's gospel, written some forty years later, the evangelist has reinterpreted the event which is why some translations report the centurion's words as: "Truly this man was the Son of God."

The Meaning of Jesus' Suffering for a Believer

Therefore, since we are surrounded by so great a cloud of witnesses, let us rid ourselves of every burden and sin that clings to us and persevere in running the race that lies before us while keeping our eyes fixed on Jesus, the leader and perfecter of faith. For the sake of the joy that lay before him he endured the cross, despising its shame, and has taken his seat at the right of the throne of God. Consider how he endured such opposition from sinners, in order that you may not grow weary and lose heart. In your struggle against sin you have not yet resisted to the point of shedding blood. You have also forgotten the exhortation addressed to you as sons:

"My son, do not disdain the discipline of the Lord
    or lose heart when reproved by him;
for whom the Lord loves, he disciplines;
    he scourges every son he acknowledges."

Endure your trials as "discipline"; God treats you as sons. For what "son" is there whom his father does not discipline? If you are without discipline, in which all have shared, you are not sons but bastards. Besides this, we have had our earthly fathers to discipline us, and we respected them. Should we not [then] submit all the more to the Father of spirits and live? They disciplined us for a short time as seemed right to them, but he does so for our benefit, in order that we may

> share his holiness. At the time, all discipline seems a cause
> not for joy but for pain, yet later it brings the peaceful fruit of
> righteousness to those who are trained by it.
>
> So strengthen your drooping hands and your weak knees.
> Make straight paths for your feet, that what is lame may not
> be dislocated but healed (Heb 12:1-13).

Though included among the letters of Paul, most likely he was not the author of Hebrews. Neither is it a letter. Hebrews is most likely a written homily, perhaps from 80–90 C.E. Earlier in this homily (Heb 5:7-10) the author reflects on the agony of Jesus noting that he prayed that God might "save him from death." His prayer was received, but God had a different plan. The sacred author's reflection in Heb 5:8 is often translated from a Western, modern faith perspective: "Son though he was, he learned obedience from what he suffered." This sentiment is likely familiar to many readers: even though he was Son (of God), he learned obedience through his suffering. In the light of what we have considered in this chapter, the Greek particle *kaiper,* traditionally translated as "though" or "although," should be more appropriately translated "precisely because" (which is one of that Greek particle's meanings). "Precisely because he was a son, he learned obedience by what he suffered," just like all Mediterranean sons.

Chapter 12 draws a practical-life application from Jesus' experience of suffering. The sacred author exhorts his readers to perseverance and proposes Jesus as a model. He despised the shame of the cross and won a place at the right of the throne of God, a prominent location. And this was, of course, God's will. The sacred author quotes Proverbs 3:11-12 to support his exhortation. Careful reflective reading of that citation will probably shock modern believers: the Lord (God) disciplines (always in its physical sense) those he loves (???), and scourges every son he acknowledges (???).

It is important to remember a basic principle from the classical, neo-Scholastic tradition: all theology is analogy. Everything human beings think and say about God (theology = God-talk) is based on human experience (analogy). And all human experience is culture-specific. God-talk in the Bible inescapably reflects Middle Eastern culture.

Proverbs 3:11-12 illustrates this admirably, and as the sacred author proceeds, he explains how. All sons are physically disciplined by their fathers. If a father is not disciplining his son, that is a sure sign that son is illegitimate. The father is not his real father. Since we had earthly, Mediterranean fathers to discipline us, should we not expect our heavenly Father to do the same?

Of course, modern Western believers will bristle at this and rightly reject it. This chapter's reflections paint in stark strokes the challenge of interpreting the Bible respectfully yet adapting it to other cultures. To its credit, the Revised New American Bible New Testament quoted here has retained "sons" in this segment of Hebrews. The reasoning about God is based entirely on the cultural experience of how earthly Mediterranean fathers physically discipline their sons. Inclusive language translations have replaced "sons" with "children." Unwittingly, such translations give biblical fundamentalists biblical "permission" for physically disciplining girls as well as boys, something completely unthinkable among our Mediterranean ancestors in the faith.

Anthropologists also caution against describing this violent treatment of sons by their fathers as "abuse." Abuse in one culture is often virtue in another. From this anthropological perspective, abuse becomes a term similar to others that express the superiority of one culture to another. The Mediterranean cultural context of the Bible provides non-Mediterranean readers with a golden opportunity to avoid the temptation of cultural triumphalism or a sense of advanced enlightenment.

Chapter Three

Jesus Announces the Reign of God

At the age of thirty, Jesus began his ministry (Luke 3:23). This was an old age in antiquity. Those who reached it were generally in poor health, suffering dental problems, poor eyesight (particularly trachoma which could lead to blindness), and malnutrition, among other things. Jesus was very likely older than the majority of the people with whom he associated or to whom he spoke. If one follows the story line of the Synoptic Gospels, Jesus' ministry probably lasted one "dry" season, the period from the end of April to the end of September in Palestine. When the "rainy" season began, everyone went back to their homes and occupations. At the beginning of the next "dry" season, Jesus went with his followers for the feast of Passover to Jerusalem where he was put to death.

Jesus, a Holy Man in the Israelite Tradition

It happened in those days that Jesus came from Nazareth of Galilee and was baptized in the Jordan by John. On coming up out of the water he saw the heavens being torn open and the Spirit, like a dove, descending upon him. And a voice came from the heavens, "You are my beloved Son; with you I am well pleased" (Mark 1:9-11).

As we already noted in Chapter 1 with regard to Joseph, the Israelite tradition recognized two kinds of righteous or "holy men." A *ṣaddiq* was an ordinary person who did his best to observe the law of God. A *ḥasid* was so concerned with pleasing God that he went beyond the basics. If it was necessary to wash one's hands before eating in order to please God, the *ṣaddiq* might be satisfied with washing the palms, but the *ḥasid* might wash up to and beyond the elbow just to be sure he met the obligation (see Mark 7:1-5). One would surely expect Jesus to be a holy man as Joseph was. As Sirach noted: "At the father's death, he will seem not dead, / since he leaves after him one like himself" (Sir 30:4). In Western culture, the saying is: "Like father, like son." Indeed, in Jesus' first recorded encounter with a possessed person, the possessing demon acknowledges Jesus' identity: "What have you to do with us, Jesus of Nazareth? Have you come to destroy us? I know who you are—the Holy One of God!" (Mark 1:24).

The baptism of Jesus precedes this encounter with the demon. Jesus is moved to repentance by the preaching of John and submits to his baptism. Perhaps his manual labor was sometimes less than perfect, perhaps he cheated a customer even if unintentionally. John was announcing "forgiveness of sins" using a word, forgive, which in peasant experience was always linked with forgiveness of debts. Even Jesus as an artisan could plausibly have needed forgiveness of debts. At the same time, John's baptism inserted the candidate into a transformed community which John announces. Meeting John in a wilderness setting, at the Jordan, means Jesus had to leave village and family behind. This is his first symbolic step out of his kinship network on the way to establishing a new, surrogate kinship network (Mark 3:33-35).

The baptism of Jesus is his formal calling and initiation as a holy man. Cross-cultural studies identify six steps in this process. One, the candidate makes contact with the spirit; two, the spirit identifies itself. Here the sky is torn open and "wind" or the spirit descends upon Jesus. Wind or spirit designates God's activity in the Bible. In verse 8 the activity of God is judgment, separating people. In verse 11, God' s activity is adopting Jesus as son. The cultural significance of this scene is that God is ascribing an otherwise unimaginable honor to Jesus. As son of Joseph, Jesus has little claim to honor, but as son of God Jesus has every right to speak and behave as he will in the rest of the gospel.

Three, the Holy Man has to acquire necessary ritual skills. The principal activity of holy men in all cultures is healing. Some are also capable of controlling spirits. The gospel story line gives evidence that Jesus is active in healing people and in casting out demons. Indeed, in the very next story about Jesus, the testing of his fidelity to the Father, Jesus demonstrates his ability to deal successfully with a malicious spirit without being harmed. Four, the Holy Man is usually an apprentice to both a spirit teacher and a human teacher. Scholars note that Jesus initially was a disciple of John, even baptizing others with the baptism of John (John 3:22). No doubt he also learned the basic skills of a Holy Man from John, an experienced, successful, and, to judge by the crowds he attracted, highly respected Holy Man.

Five, once initiated, the Holy Man becomes increasingly familiar with the adopting spirit and the spirit world. This is certainly evident in the Transfiguration of Jesus in which Jesus is again acknowledged by God as "my beloved son" and the disciples-witnesses are instructed to "listen to him" more so than to Moses and Elijah in that scene (Mark 9:2-87). Finally, the Holy Man continues to have other experiences similar to the call and initiation experience which can be technically described as a real experience in an altered state of consciousness. Because God and the spirit world are involved in this experience, anthropologists call it a "religious trance." In the life of Jesus, these would include the testing (Mark 1:12-13); walking on the sea (Mark 6:45-52); the Transfiguration (Mark 9:2-8). For his followers, all experiences of the Risen Jesus are instances of "religious trance."

The Testing of Jesus

> Filled with the holy Spirit, Jesus returned from the Jordan and was led by the Spirit into the desert for forty days, to be tempted by the devil. He ate nothing during those days, and

when they were over he was hungry. The devil said to him, "If you are the Son of God, command this stone to become bread." Jesus answered him, "It is written, 'One does not live by bread alone.'" Then he took him up and showed him all the kingdoms of the world in a single instant. The devil said to him, "I shall give to you all this power and their glory; for it has been handed over to me, and I may give it to whomever I wish. All this will be yours, if you worship me." Jesus said to him in reply, "It is written:

'You shall worship the Lord, your God,
   and him alone shall you serve.'"

Then he led him to Jerusalem, made him stand on the parapet of the temple, and said to him, "If you are the Son of God, throw yourself down from here, for it is written:

'He will command his angels concerning you,
   to guard you,'

and:

'With their hands they will support you,
   lest you dash your foot against a stone.'"

Jesus said to him in reply, "It also says, 'You shall not put the Lord, your God, to the test.'" When the devil had finished every temptation, he departed from him for a time (Luke 4:1-13).

In a culture where honor is the core value, every honor claim or grant of honor is definitely going to be tested by others. In Mark's report of the baptism, God ascribes to Jesus the honor of being favored by the deity. The many spirits who densely populate the air have heard that compliment. Every Mediterranean person knows what to expect next. Someone is going to test that honor, perhaps even try to disprove it. Beloved son? Loyal to the Father? Well, we'll just see about that.

Mark's brief report (1:12-13) says quite simply that Jesus was "tempted by Satan." Matthew and Luke report three temptations, though in different order. This longer report was drawn by each of these two evangelists from the hypothetical sayings-source which scholars call "Q" (from the German word for spring or source: *Quelle*). This source is central to the Two Source hypothesis, the other source being

Mark's Gospel. Thus, in its simplest form, the hypothesis claims that when the Synoptic Gospels all report the same saying or story (e.g., that John baptized Jesus), Mark served as the source for Matthew and Luke. But when both Matthew and Luke report the same saying or story that is *not* reported by Mark (e.g., the three tests of Jesus), these evangelists drew it from "Q."

The reader will notice that we do not use the word "temptations" but rather the word "tests." The modern understanding of "temptation" carries centuries of theological freight which make it difficult to understand Jesus' experience. As already noted, these are "tests" of Jesus' reputation as beloved son ascribed by God in his baptism. A beloved Mediterranean son is one who is loyal to his father. Hence these are tests of Jesus' loyalty.

The fact that Satan is involved confirms the notion of "testing" as preferable to "temptations." Satan is a concept that derives from the Persian period (post–537 B.C.E.). The ruler sent out "spies" (satans) who would dress like the local peasants, blend in with them, and then ask questions about the ruler. If the peasant was duped into speaking critical judgments about the ruler, the spy would reveal himself and cart the peasant off to jail. The peasant was guilty of lack of loyalty. When King Abdullah Hussein of Jordan succeeded his father not long ago, he often would put on a beard and shabby clothing, mix in with the people, and ask for their evaluation of various government offices. When they gave their honest evaluations, he revealed his identity and thanked them for helping him to check on the efficacy and efficiency of the government.

The sequence of tests in Matthew (bread–Temple–mountain) is probably original to Q because the Scripture citations from Deuteronomy there appear in reverse orderly sequence (Deut 8:3; Deut 6:16; Deut 6:13). Luke has placed the Temple last because Temple is a major motif in his Gospel.

The report of the three tests by both evangelists is an illustration of challenge and riposte. Satan begins each challenge with "if," indicating he is not certain or convinced of Jesus' identity and ascribed honor. Perhaps he will be able to shame Jesus, make him disloyal, and thereby undo the honor. If you are the Son of God, change these stones into bread. Jesus replies by quoting Deuteronomy 8:3. In many of his discussions, particularly with experts in Torah, Jesus quotes or alludes to the Torah. He takes the argument to their turf. In this case, Satan recognizes in Jesus' riposte a new challenge to him. In his second challenge, Satan shows that he can quote from Scripture too (Ps 91:11-12). Jesus counters Satan's challenge by quoting Deuteronomy 6:16. Finally, Satan gives his third challenge, and Jesus' riposte is drawn from Deuteronomy 6:13. The end result is that Jesus not only defended his honor (reputation), but shamed his accuser who failed in three attempts. Moreover, by masterfully quoting the words of his Father, Jesus successfully defends his ascribed status as God's son. If this game is played in private, it is of no use. The public here is the reader who, fully understanding the importance of this game in Mediterranean culture, is expected by the evangelist to confirm the outcome and honor due to Jesus.

Jesus Begins to Form His Faction

> As he passed by the Sea of Galilee, he saw Simon and his brother Andrew casting their nets into the sea; they were fishermen. Jesus said to them, "Come after me, and I will make you fishers of men." Then they left their nets and followed him. He walked along a little farther and saw James, the son of Zebedee, and his brother John. They too were in a boat mending their nets. Then he called them. So they left their father Zebedee in the boat along with the hired men and followed him (Mark 1:16-20).

In Mark's story line, this is the first time Jesus has met these men. What would motivate them to leave everything and follow him? Quite likely the gossip network had already spread the word about Jesus' move from Nazareth to Capernaum, about his presence in the area, and about his agenda. It is because they know Jesus' agenda that these men are already prepared to join him. Social scientists call this activity "faction formation." In a faction, members have strong bonds with the leader but very weak bonds to one another. Recall how angry the ten became when James and John asked Jesus for privileged places in his success (Mark 10:35-45). Honor requires that one remain in the status in which one was born. It is shameful to try to improve that status as these two do here. How could they do this? Because in this setting, their primary dedication is to Jesus, the leader. They have little concern for the others.

What was Jesus' agenda? That, too, is not specified. One can conjecture that it has to do with a renewal of theocracy. "Kingdom or reign of God" describes theocracy, a situation in which God rules and God's justice would prevail for all. Peasants who lived at subsistence levels knew that taxes and tribute paid to the Temple were intended to be redistributed to the needy. Instead they recognized that Temple personnel spent the taxes and tribute on items for conspicuous consumption. Jesus as an artisan and these fishermen would surely share such concerns and would hope for reestablishing theocracy as God intended it to be.

While specific individual persons are mentioned in this pericope, Western readers must remember that our ancestors in the faith were collectivistic personalities. Each person drew identity from the group and depended upon the group to sustain that identity and status. Readers know that Simon is actually Simon bar-Jonah (Matt 16:17). As we have learned about marriage previously, a woman leaves her home and moves in with her husband, who will continue to live in his father's compound. Simon, who is married, lives with his family, including his brother Andrew and all his other single and married brothers, in the "house," or better compound, of their father, Jonah. When Jesus moved from Nazareth to Capernaum where Simon and Andrew answered his call to join the faction he was forming, Jesus was given a "room" in Jonah's compound. The same is true of James and John who live with their brothers, married and single, in the compound of their father, Zebedee. These collectivistic personalities draw their identity and strength and support from their respective families.

Collectivistic personalities do not prize individualism. In fact, individualism hardly exists in collectivistic societies which are represented in 80 percent of the current population of the planet. They tend to judge by stereotype. Notice the stereotype Mark reports: Simon and Andrew were casting their nets into the sea *because* they were fishermen. Did Mark think his audience might suspect they were tossing nets into the sea because they were vandals? Isn't their behavior in this context rather obvious? Or again when Jesus raises the twelve-year-old girl from death, Mark reports in a literal translation: "and immediately the girl arose and walked around, *for* she was twelve years old" (Mark 5:42). The girl walks because she is old enough to walk around.

In Mark's report of Jesus calling these men to join him, we also learn something about fishing. Fishing was a major industry in the first century, much too demanding to be the occupation of a single–even very extended–family. The families of Jonah and Zebedee banded together to form a "cooperative" as it were. They also employed "hired men" who remained with Zebedee when his sons left to join Jesus' faction. Jonah and Zebedee would have to hire more day laborers to replace their sons. But, if Jesus could deliver on what he promised, these patriarchs considered their short-time gamble to be well worth it. All boats rise in a rising tide.

Fishing was part of the tax network. Toll collectors, like Levi, the son of Alphaeus (Mark 1:14), bought fishing rights from the government in Jerusalem which controlled fishing. In his turn, Levi would have brokered the rights to local fishermen. Often he had to provide capital for them as well! In return for these fishing rights, cooperatives were obliged to return a percentage of the catch–sometimes as high as 40 percent! In its turn, the cooperative would be given cash or processed fish. First-century records indicate the payment was frequently irregular and inadequate. Fish became a popular item in the first-century diet of Palestine, especially among the elite of Jerusalem who lived within its walls.

Jesus Forms a Surrogate Family

> His mother and his brothers arrived. Standing outside they sent word to him and called him. A crowd seated around him told him, "Your mother and your brothers [and your sisters] are outside asking for you." But he said to them in reply, "Who are my mother and [my] brothers?" And looking around at those seated in the circle he said, "Here are my mother and my brothers. [For] whoever does the will of God is my brother and sister and mother" (Mark 3:31-35).

In the ancient (and contemporary) Mediterranean world, the large, extended family was central to a person's life. Not only did it endow members with status (ascribed honor) in the community, but it also embedded its members in an extensive economic, religious, educational, and social network. Any form of removal from the family meant a loss of connection to these life-giving networks and loss of connection to ancestral land. Those who suffered repulsive skin disorders and were thereby forced to live outside of the family and community lost such vital connections (see Lev 13:45-46). To voluntarily remove oneself from one's family is equivalent to social suicide.

In the gospel story line, Jesus left Nazareth to be baptized by John in the Jordan (Mark 1:9). Afterward, he formed a faction of the fishermen he called along the Sea of Galilee near Capernaum (Mark 1:16). As his reputation began to spread, he taught in synagogues located in Galilee, which further increased his honorable reputation. Along the way he visited his home hamlet of Nazareth, where he was not well-received. Indeed, their response to his teaching was a desire to kill him (Luke 4:14-30). Recognizing the danger he faced, his family declared him crazy, a strategy by which they could save his life (Mark 3:21). In the Middle East, breaches of honor require the death of the transgressor. A family could save the transgressor's life by declaring him crazy. But with this declaration, the transgressor cannot marry, cannot leave the family compound, cannot engage in many other activities. He might as well be dead, but at least he is a help to the family.

Jesus, however, did not wait to be rescued by his family. He found a new home with his newly-formed faction. In particular and in reality, Jesus had a "home" (place) in the same compound where Simon and Andrew lived: the home of Jonah the patriarch, father of Simon and Andrew (already as early in the gospel story as Mark 2:1).

It is to this "home" of Jesus (Mark 3:20) that his mother and brothers come, presumably to rescue him (Mark 3:32). In the revised New Testament of the New American Bible which is reported above, verse 32 contains a verse in brackets: and your sisters. The use of brackets indicates that this is a "doubtful reading of some merit." This means that among the ancient Greek manuscripts we possess, some contain the passage while others do not. The NAB considers it worth keeping because the lack of that phrase in verses 31, 33, and 34 suggests that Jesus did say it in verse 32, and it would be easily, even if unintentionally, omitted by scribe-copyists. The New Revised Standard Version Bible reports that same phrase in its text without brackets, but mentions in a footnote that "other ancient authorities," the customary reference to Greek manuscripts, report it. The New Jerusalem Bible reports it in the text without brackets and offers no footnote at that point.

The revised NAB translation is quite likely a good decision shared by other translations as well. The insight that Mediterranean cultural perspective offers is this: how did the family gather outside? Were they standing as a mixed group? Not very likely. It is more plausible that adult males were separate from the younger males and the women of Jesus' family who would have been clustered around Mary. Given the strong emotional bond that exists between mother and eldest son (stronger than the bond between husband and wife, and surpassed in intensity only by the bond between brother and sister), Mary fully expects Jesus to respond to her summons.

What is startling in Mark's report is that there is no indication Jesus obeyed. Indeed, his comment "when told of her summons" carries an unmistakable though quite understandable harsh tone. The intensely close relationship between mother and son was often considered to be suffocating. Thus Jesus, in his actual lifetime, is building a surrogate family to replace the family he left behind in Nazareth. In the evangelist's lifetime (ca. 69 C.E.), however, the believing community recognizes that it serves as a surrogate family to all those who have left behind their family of origin to embrace Jesus as Messiah. This surrogate family transcends all the familiar Mediterranean categories of birth, status, race, gender, education, wealth, and power. Those who abandon their family of origin and join the surrogate family of believers had, in Mark's report, incredibly great rewards: "a hundred times more now in this present age: houses and brothers and sisters and mothers and children and lands, with persecutions, and eternal life in the age to come" (Mark 10:30).

Parables: Jesus Says One Thing, but Means Something Else

The parables are Jesus' way of revealing information about God. The phrase "the kingdom of heaven [or the reign of God] is like . . ." means this is how life is when God is really in charge. In other words, the following parable is not about vineyards, employer-employee relationships, social justice, or anything of the sort. While the story centers on a landowner and workers he hires to tend his vineyard, it is really about God.

God as Generous Patron

The kingdom of heaven is like a landowner who went out at dawn to hire laborers for his vineyard. After agreeing with them for the usual daily wage, he sent them into his vineyard. Going out about nine o'clock, he saw others standing idle in the marketplace, and he said to them, "You too go into my vineyard, and I will give you what is just." So they went off. [And] he went out again around noon, and around three o'clock, and did likewise. Going out about five o'clock, he found others standing around, and said to them, "Why do you stand here idle all day?" They answered, "Because no one has hired us." He said to them, "You too go into my vineyard." When it was evening the owner of the vineyard said to his foreman, "Summon the laborers and give them their pay, beginning with the last and ending with the first." When those who had started about five o'clock came, each received the usual daily wage. So when the first came, they thought that they would receive more, but each of them also got the usual wage. And on receiving it they grumbled against the land-owner, saying, "These last ones worked only one hour, and you have made them equal to us, who bore the day's burden and the heat." He said to one of them in reply, "My friend, I am not cheating you. Did you not agree with me for the usual daily wage? Take what is yours and go. What if I wish to give this last one the same as you? [Or] am I not free to do as I wish with my own money? Are you envious because I am generous?" Thus, the last will be first, and the first will be last (Matt 20:1-16).

To understand Matthew's parable (no other evangelist reports this story), a reader must be familiar with three distinctive concepts in Mediterranean culture: the peasant view known as limited good; the social institution known as patronage; and the evil eye. Peasants routinely live at a subsistence level and never know where the next meal is coming from, or whether there will even be a next meal. Hence peasants believe that all the desirable and necessary goods of this world (food, gold, honor, etc.) are finite in quantity and already distributed. In the peasant view, "there is no more where this came from." Each person should be satisfied with what they have and not strive to augment or improve it. Such behavior is shameful because in this view of life, if one person gets more another person now has less. In modern terms, peasant life is a zero-sum game.

Notice that no one asks the landowner for work. It would be shameful to ask for work. How dare anyone imagine that someone else owes them something, like a job? These men stand around waiting to be invited. Such behavior is rooted in the belief that all goods are finite in quantity and already distributed. The landowner goes out five times during the work day to invite these day laborers to work in his vineyard.

The landowner is a patron. This means that he is a person of means, a person who has surplus. In this culture, such a person is obliged to distribute his surplus to those in need. Surplus is not something to save for one's personal rainy day (see Luke 12:16-21). A person with surplus is, however, free to select the needy people for whom he will be a patron. It can be based entirely on whim. In other words, a patron freely chooses to treat complete strangers as if they were his family. He will treat them favorably, indeed with favoritism.

The last concept is "evil eye." To appreciate this concept, readers must recognize that our Mediterranean ancestors in the faith were not only non-introspective but anti-introspective. They did not believe human beings could look into the hearts of others and understand them or their motivations. They judged other human beings entirely by outward appearances (see 1 Sam 16:7). They identified three zones on the human body which they endowed with symbolic meaning. The heart-eyes zone represents emotion-fused thinking. Human beings have eyes to gather information and send it to the heart for processing, reflection, judgment. "And his mother [Mary] kept all these things in her heart" (Luke 2:51) when she and Joseph returned to Nazareth with the boy Jesus from the Passover trip to Jerusalem. The mouth-ears zone represents self-expressive speech. Human beings have ears to learn about others on the basis of what they share. They have mouths to similarly share, though of course the sharing can be deceptive or misleading. Finally, the hands-feet zone represents purposeful activity. When all zones work harmoniously, the person is healthy and whole. When one or another zone malfunctions (e.g., blindness or being mute), such a person is ill and needs healing.

In Western culture, if someone sees his neighbor's new Cadillac and admires it, he may be moved to purchase a new car for himself. No doubt it will be a better car, perhaps a BMW or a Mercedes. In Western culture, there is always more where this came from! But in a world of limited good where people believe there is no more where this came from, admiring the cherished possession of another person can lead to desiring it. To take it from the other person would be shameful! The desire doesn't die, however, and so the eye which feeds this information to the heart is then prompted by the heart to turn evil and cast a destructive gaze at the prized object. (Recall Jesus' warning: "If your eye causes you to sin [= is evil], tear it out and throw it away," Matt 18:9; Mark 9:47.)

In Mediterranean culture of antiquity and the present, the evil eye is associated with and often translated by the word "envy." Someone envious of another person's good health can, by giving that person "the fierce look," ruin that health. Amulets and gestures were used to protect against the evil eye. The blue tassels on cloaks and prayer shawls were also worn as protection against the evil eye (Matt 18:20).

Now we are prepared to understand Jesus' parable. The landowner goes out to hire day laborers five times during the day. He agrees on a contract with the first hired but tells the others, "I will give you what is just" (Matt 20:4). At the end of the day the foreman pays the workers beginning with the last hired, who receive a denarius. They trusted the landowner and received over and beyond what is just. The first hired also receive a denarius, which is what they agreed upon with the landowner and is just. Suddenly the first hired recognize that the landowner has acted with them as employer to employee on the basis of an agreed contract, but he has acted with the others as patron to clients. He has treated them "as if" they were his blood relatives. He has treated them with favoritism.

The first hired are understandably furious. Their response is to give the landowner and his vineyard the "evil eye." The landowner asks them pointedly: "Are you envious because I am generous?" The literal translation of the Greek is: "Is your eye evil because I am generous?" (Matt 20:15). In other words, the first hired, who have been given the just payment for which they contracted, now wish evil on the landowner and the vineyard. If we recall that this story is not about landowners, vineyards, and workers, but rather about God and how God interacts with people, isn't it rather risky to give God the evil eye? To wish God destruction because others seem more favored by God than those who believe they drove a bargain with God?

God's behavior should surprise no one. "I loved Jacob but hated Esau," says God (Mal 1:3). The meaning of this sentence is that God preferred the second born, Jacob, to the firstborn, Esau. Of course God knows the divinely determined rights of the firstborn as recorded by Moses (Deut 21:15-17). Since God determined these rights, God can change them. Paul quotes Malachi too when reflecting on the position of Israel relative to Gentiles in God's plan. Then he adds: "What then are we to say? Is there injustice on the part of God? Of course not!" (Rom 9:14).

Matthew 20:15 quite likely is the original ending of Jesus' parable. Since every parable has only one point, this is exactly the point Jesus was making about God. Is God not free to do what God wills, no matter how unfair or whimsical it may seem to some of God's creatures? The evangelist or his sources may have added verse 16: "Thus the last will be first, and the first will be last." It doesn't make a fit ending to the story, since if the workers were paid in the order in which they were hired, the first hired would likely not have stayed to witness what the others would receive. But the verse does form an "inclusion" with Matthew 19:30. An "inclusion" is a literary device used by an author to identify a discrete unit in his composition. It is formed by the repetition of words or phrases which signal the beginning and end of a text-segment. For Matthew, these verses (19:30 and 20:16) serve as two pieces of bread that "sandwich" the enclosed verses into his Gospel.

At level two of interpretation (the apostles, 30–69 C.E.), verse 16 about the last and the first could have been a "floating saying" repeated by preachers to explain the influx of non-Israelites who accepted Jesus as Messiah, and to explain why some—perhaps the majority—of Israelites rejected Jesus as Messiah. At level three of interpretation (Matthew, 85 C.E.), verse 16 could represent the community's response to being formally ejected from the synagogues for accepting Jesus as Messiah beginning around the year 80 C.E. Those who once were chosen but are now kicking us out of the synagogues will be last. (Recall the statement reflecting Matthew's time [85 C.E.] rather than Jesus' [30 C.E.] at the beginning of this Gospel: Jesus "went around all of Galilee, teaching in their synagogues," Matt 4:23.)

Jesus Laments the Widow's Behavior

> When he looked up he saw some wealthy people putting their offerings into the treasury and he noticed a poor widow putting in two small coins. He said, "I tell you truly, this poor widow put in more than all the rest; for those others have all made offerings from their surplus wealth, but she, from her poverty, has offered her whole livelihood" (Luke 21:1-4).

It is important to read this story from the peasant perspective of limited good. Since all goods are finite in quantity and already distributed, it is impossible to obtain more goods "honestly." At the same time, one must safeguard what one has. If one loses it and cannot find it, there is no more where this came from.

The word for "widow" in Hebrew carries the meaning of one who is silent, unable to speak. In the gender-divided Mediterranean world, men interact in the public sphere; women stay secluded along with the children deep within the home where they manage household affairs. Men play the public role and speak in public; women do not speak on their own behalf.

By definition, a widow has already lost one significant male in her life: her husband. Every Mediterranean woman is always under the care of one of three men: her father, her brother, and/or her husband. If her father is dead, that leaves only the possibility of a son. If the widow in this story still has an unmarried eldest son, who is going to arrange the marriage? If she has no son at all, she might have to return to her family of origin (see Lev 22:13; Ruth 1:8), if indeed that were still an option. Among the early followers of Jesus, widows were a major concern. Younger ones were urged to remarry (1 Tim 5:3-16, esp. v. 14).

Because widows were not included in Israelite inheritance laws, they were deeply concerned with how to live day by day. Whatever resources this widow might have had would have been very meager. Her cultural obligation, like every one else in this society, was to maintain her status and not to do anything to jeopardize it or lessen it. As a widow, she has already lost a notch in status. If Jesus' observation is accurate, that this widow has given to the Temple "her whole liveli-hood," then she has acted very foolishly and shamefully. She has deliberately worsened her status. On another occasion, Jesus condemned the making of donations to the Temple and thereby depriving one's parents of support (Mark 7:10-13). It would be doubly wrong for an adult, a widow with no other apparent source of support, to give away the little she has and plunge herself irretrievably into deeper poverty.

No, Jesus does not praise this woman. He rather laments her behavior. He directs his scathing scorn toward the scribes, those experts in the Law of Moses who taught and encouraged this kind of shameful behavior to such as this widow (see Luke 20:45-47). Jesus criticizes the scribes for their ostentatious—and expensive!—robes, their grasping for honor (greetings in the market place), and active partici-pation in "places of honor at banquets." To attend a banquet means one must invite the host to a banquet in return. All these criticisms involve access to wealth. Where did the scribes find such resources?

The Temple tribute that was collected from all Israelites was intended to be redistributed by Temple personnel to the poor and needy. It wasn't at all. Instead it was hoarded and used for behaviors of conspicuous consumption as noted. Moreover, the wealth was unjustly acquired by deceiving people such as this poor widow. That phrase is almost tauta-logical. Poor describes someone who has temporarily lost status. A widow has lost status as a married person embed-ded in a husband and his family. With devoted obedience, she has listened to the misleading teachings of the scribes who, Jesus says, "devour the houses of widows" (Luke 20:47). Indeed, no sooner has Jesus completed his criticism of the scribes when a widow comes along to fulfill her Tem-ple duty and makes Jesus' point.

If this interpretation is difficult to accept, and one prefers to say that Jesus is praising this widow for her sacrifi-cial spirit of giving, the story that follows then portrays Jesus as heartless and cruel (Luke 21:5-36). Jesus says of the beau-tiful Jerusalem Temple: "All that you see here—the days will come when there will not be left a stone upon another stone that will not be thrown down." Would Jesus in one breath praise the widow for despoiling herself to contribute to the Temple yet in the next breath say that this Temple will soon be destroyed? That is not very likely. It is indeed much more likely that Jesus is lamenting this woman's behavior misguided as it was by the teaching of the scribes.

Chapter Four

Jesus Seeks to Establish the Reign of God

The key activities by which Jesus sought to establish the reign of God were teaching, preaching, but most especially healing. Healing is the restoration of meaning to life. Curing is the destruction or control of pathogens that cause disease. We have very slim evidence for cures in the ancient world. Without microscopes, laboratory tests, CAT scans, and similar scientific tools, it is difficult to know the precise nature of illnesses described in the Bible. But the evidence is clear that many people found new meaning in life as a result of their encounter with a healer. In the Bible, God is the healer, and God is also the one who sends sickness (see Exod 15:26). With the spread of Greek medicine after Alexander's conquests, the Israelites had to consider the role of human physicians in human well-being. Sirach (38:1-15) reflects the ambivalence that conservative Israelites felt toward physicians. Yes, they can help, but actually God heals. Yes, they prescribe medications, but God created the medications. In this chapter, let us reflect on human life in New Testament times and the way in which Jesus tried to restore meaning to the lives of those with whom he associated.

Jesus the Healer as Broker

When he had finished all his words to the people, he entered Capernaum. A centurion there had a slave who was ill and about to die, and he was valuable to him. When he heard about Jesus, he sent elders of the Jews to him, asking him to come and save the life of his slave. They approached Jesus and strongly urged him to come, saying, "He deserves to have you do this for him, for he loves our nation and he built the synagogue for us." And Jesus went with them, but when he was only a short distance from the house, the centurion sent friends to tell him, "Lord, do not trouble yourself, for I am not worthy to have you enter under my roof. Therefore, I did not consider myself worthy to come to you; but say the word and let my servant be healed. For I too am a person subject to authority, with soldiers subject to me. And I say to one, 'Go,' and he goes; and to another, 'Come here,' and he comes; and to my slave, 'Do this,' and he does it." When Jesus heard this he was amazed at him and, turning, said to the crowd following him, "I tell you, not even in Israel have I found such faith." When the messengers returned to the house, they found the slave in good health (Luke 7:1-10).

The key to understanding this story and Jesus' role as a first-century healer is the Mediterranean institution known as "patronage." In the Mediterranean world of antiquity, central government was perceived by the people to be ineffectual in meeting their needs. They had to look after their own needs. Peasants could do this in two ways. One, the way of mutual obligation: "I do you a favor. Now you owe me a favor. When you return the favor, I owe you another, in a never-ending process." This is called a dyadic contract, a form of balanced reciprocity. Two, the way of recourse to a patron, that is, someone who can obtain for the client whatever the client could not obtain by personal effort, or on better terms than could be obtained by personal effort. When one's social equals cannot come through, one has recourse to a "social superior," that is, a patron.

The centurion in this story represents Rome to the local community. He is an intermediary who brokers favors and resources from Rome to the local citizenry. The fact that he has provided funds for the construction of a synagogue also means he is a patron. The delegation to Jesus is correct in saying "he loves our nation." A patron by definition freely chooses his clients and freely elects to treat them as if they were family, personally related. This is what family love in the Mediterranean world entails.

The local Judean elders are connected with the synagogue, perhaps as the "board of elders" that administered the community's affairs. As such they are "clients" of the centurion. They are in his debt for building the synagogue.

It is easy to understand that one way of honoring their patron, the centurion, is for the elders to become "middlemen" or "go-betweens" with Jesus on behalf of the centurion. Their role is simply that of messengers: they bring the centurion's request to Jesus and hope for a favorable response. In Jesus' presence, these elders fulfill another common obligation of a client: they sing the praises of their patron to Jesus. Since this meeting is quite public, everyone hears about the good qualities of the centurion, who loves these people and treats them as if they were family.

The centurion desires a healing intervention from Jesus on behalf of his sick slave. By sending a second delegation, "friends," to Jesus with a special message: "don't bother to come under my roof," the centurion masterfully employs additional key elements in the culture to spell out his relationship to Jesus. The centurion sees Jesus as a "social superior." After all, the centurion is not a native; he is a resident alien capable of brokering imperial privilege and commanding a small entourage. But Jesus, the healing-prophet, is a native of this country. As a prophet and healer in Israel, Jesus is a broker between the God of Israel and God's sick people.

Outsiders, like the centurion, see Jesus as a powerful patron. It would be awkward for one powerful patron to interact with another powerful patron. The risk of shame would be high, because one of these would be made to look like the other one's client. The centurion is well aware and does not intend to project this challenge, hence he relies on go-betweens like the Judean elders who are his clients and personal friends (who by definition are obligated to him) to intercede for him with Jesus.

In particular, the centurion recognizes something that the Israelites refuse to see: Jesus' authority or power to heal (see Luke 20:2). Jesus' response to the centurion's friends spells it out explicitly: "Truly, not even in Israel have I found faith or loyalty like this!" The centurion's slave is healed.

The behavior of the centurion toward Jesus helps a reader to understand how this very basic idea of patronage undergirds all of life in the Mediterranean world, including its understanding of healers and healing. Notice that Luke does not say Jesus healed the slave. God is the healer, Jesus is God's broker who puts clients (sick people) in touch with the patron (God).

Jesus Restores Meaning to Life

A leper came to him [and kneeling down] begged him and said, "If you wish, you can make me clean." Moved with pity, he stretched out his hand, touched him, and said to him, "I do will it. Be made clean." The leprosy left him immediately, and he was made clean. Then, warning him sternly, he dismissed him at once. Then he said to him, "See that you tell no one anything, but go, show yourself to the priest and offer for your cleansing what Moses prescribed; that will be proof for them." The man went away and began to publicize the whole matter. He spread the report abroad so that it was impossible for Jesus to enter a town openly. He remained outside in deserted places, and people kept coming to him from everywhere (Mark 1:40-45).

No bones from antiquity containing evidence of true leprosy (Hansen's disease) have yet been found in Israel. Leprous bones found in Egypt date from the third century C.E. Further, the Hebrew and Greek words in the Bible which are translated as "leprosy" do not describe true leprosy. Rather, they describe something like a scaly condition, sometimes repulsive, that affects the skin (Leviticus 13), garments (Lev 14:47-59), or the walls of houses (Lev 14:33-53). What then is the real problem?

Notice the way in which the sick person describes his problem in Mark's report. He wants to be made clean, hence his problem is that he is unclean, dirty, impure, not holy. Jesus takes his request seriously and says: "Be made clean." The man is no longer unclean. Jesus did not say: "I cleanse you," or "I pronounce you clean." He uses the passive voice, which is the customary way in the Bible of talking about God without using God's name. When no human agent can be identified, the passive voice points to God as the agent. God cleansed this petitioner.

The lengthy discussions in Leviticus 13–14 all concern the determination of whether a person with this condition ("leprosy") is clean or unclean. This focus reflects a concern for purity and holiness. Throughout Leviticus, God reminds the people: "Be holy (pure, sacred, etc.), for I, the Lord, your God, am holy" (19:2). A person like the man with the skin condition who approached Jesus was unclean, therefore impure, not holy, not sacred. His punishment: "He shall dwell apart, making his abode outside the camp" (Lev 13:46). For a collectivistic personality who draws his identity, strength, and support from the community, being forced to live outside of it is like a death sentence.

If we expand our view to include Leviticus 11–15, all of which concern various clean and unclean things and conditions, we can gain a better understanding of the problem. All these chapters deal with body-openings and the dangers they pose to being clean. The food laws (Leviticus 11) identify unclean foods, the eating of which will render the person unclean. Childbirth (Leviticus 12) sets a normal body opening at risk. Unusual openings on the body, garments, and walls (Leviticus 13–14) also render these things vulnerable to pollution. Even normal, involuntary body emissions (Leviticus 15) render a person unclean and require purification. There is a concern for boundaries, maintaining secure boundaries, and potential breaches of the boundaries in these chapters.

Dirt, by definition, is matter out of place, that is, it is outside of the boundaries within which it belongs. It doesn't belong where it is found. There it is considered "dirt" and "dirty." It has a proper place, elsewhere. Drawing an analogy from this concept, our ancestors in the faith had an idea of what it means to be pure, clean, holy as God is holy. Any deviation from that idea made one impure, unclean, and not holy, and threatened God's holy community. Such a one was like "dirt" or "dirty" and had to be removed from the community lest it become displeasing to God.

These specific rules in Leviticus began to be strictly enforced during the Exile. Officials informed Ezra: "Neither the Israelite laymen nor the priests nor the Levites have kept themselves aloof from the peoples of the land and their abominations . . . ; for they have taken some of their daughters as wives for themselves and their sons, and thus they have desecrated the holy race with the peoples of the land" (Ezra 9:1-2). Some Israelites introduced "dirt" into the holy boundaries of Israel. These people were not holy and did not properly belong in God's holy community. Ezra's decision: "Now, give praise to the LORD, the God of your fathers, and do his will: separate yourselves from the peoples of the land and from these foreign women" (Ezra 10:11).

In all cultures, rules that govern the physical body are replicated in the social body as well. Thus, Ezra's concern for restoring the holiness of God's people directed him to order the breakup of marriages with foreign women. To reinforce the concern for communal purity in the social body, the rules governing clean and unclean foods were also enforced so that the physical human body would be pure. Both would thus be pleasing and holy to God.

When Jesus touches the leper, at least two things take place. One, power is exercised in his healing touch. A debatable skin condition improves. Two, by touching him Jesus demonstrates that the man is not polluting as Leviticus asserts. (Real leprosy is minimally contagious. Spouses rarely contract it from the afflicted partner.) The man is no threat to God's holy community, and Jesus' touch signifies bringing the man back into community. Recall that he was to live outside the community. He took a risk to encounter Jesus, and it paid off.

Jesus the Healer and the Sick people, His Clients

After he left the synagogue, he entered the house of Simon. Simon's mother-in-law was afflicted with a severe fever, and they interceded with him about her. He stood over her, rebuked the fever, and it left her. She got up immediately and waited on them.

> At sunset, all who had people sick with various diseases brought them to him. He laid his hands on each of them and cured them (Luke 4:38-40).

In this English translation (and many other translations), there are two problematic words: "diseases" and "cured." To read and interpret our Bible respectfully, we have been encouraging the use of Mediterranean lenses. In matters of human health and sickness, the modern understanding of "disease" and "cure" is not applicable to the ancient world. In the modern world, a fever is not a disease. It may or may not be a symptom. Sometimes a rise in body temperature can be quite normal. Some deeper stages of consciousness are accompanied by a rise in temperature.

The clue to understanding this report about Peter's mother-in-law is that Jesus "rebuked the fever." Only Luke reports this (compare Matt 8:14-15; Mark 1:29-31). Just prior to this event, Luke reports that Jesus rebuked an unclean spirit he was casting out of a possessed man in the synagogue at Capernaum (4:35). After healing Peter's mother-in-law, when Jesus was healing various people, demons came out of many identifying him: "You are the Son of God," but he rebuked them (4:41). When they were caught in a storm on the Sea of Galilee, Jesus rebuked the wind = spirit (8:24). Finally, Jesus rebuked the unclean spirit who possessed a boy and threw him on the ground (9:42). The significance of Luke's use of "rebuke" in these instances is that he believes Peter's mother-in-law was possessed by a spirit named Fever. Jesus successfully casts the demon out because he is a holy man, recognized as such by the demons (Luke 4:34).

The Testament of Solomon, a third-century C.E. document, reflects beliefs and practices of first-century Palestinian Judaism fairly accurately. The author's interest was predominantly in sickness problems of that time. Some are associated with heavenly bodies or spirits, and the author provides assorted remedies or exorcistic words. Thus he reports: "The sixteenth [heavenly body, or demon] said: 'I am Katrax. I inflict incurable fevers on [human beings]. If anyone wants to regain health, let [that one] pulverize coriander and rub it on the lips, saying, 'I adjure you by Zeus, retreat from the image of God,' and I retreat immediately" (Test. Sol. 18:20).

Mediterranean culture contributes still other insights to the understanding and interpretation of this healing report. The first question is: What is Peter's mother-in-law doing in Peter's house? If the ideal marriage partner is a patrilateral cousin, and marriage consists in the groom (Peter) fetching that female cousin (his wife) and bringing her to live with him in his father Jonah's compound, the wife's mother would remain in her own home. If she is now sick in Peter's house, it is plausible that her husband has died and she has no sons (or brother) to take care of her.

A second point to notice is that as soon as she is healed, "she got up immediately and waited on them" (Luke 4:39). When men are healed in the gospel stories, they usually go out and tell others, immediately. This is an understandable spontaneous response. Why did Peter's mother-in-law not do the same? In this culture men's primary response to all situations is spontancity, whatever the moment calls for. Women in this culture run the household, which involves planned and calculated activity. That in general is the Mediterranean woman's primary response. Serving them is a planned and calculated activity. It involves having provisions on hand, preparing them, and serving them to guests. In all cultures, the dominant value represents the dominant male value. In ancient Israel, this was spontaneity. A secondary or perhaps even tertiary value for men would be planned and calculated activity. But for women in ancient Israel, planned and calculated activity is their primary value. Spontaneity for women is secondary.

There is yet a third cultural point to observe. Some scholars have argued that the success of the Jesus movement and subsequent Jesus groups lies in the care they extended to the sick. In particular, say these scholars, this health care was free. However, nothing in the Mediterranean world is free. An Arab proverb that captures millennia of Mediterranean behavior says: "Don't thank me. You *will* repay me." Again we encounter balanced reciprocity in the form of a dyadic contract. I do you a favor, you repay me, I repay you, on and on until one of us is no longer able.

Jesus does the mother-in-law a favor: he casts out the demon Fever. She owes him and repays immediately by serving him. In the next chapter (Luke 5:1-3), Jesus is feeling crowded at the lake of Gennesaret and wants to escape. He sees two empty boats and steps into Peter's. Did Peter give him permission? How dare Jesus presume? He healed Peter's mother-in-law which was also a favor for Peter; Peter owed Jesus, so Jesus borrowed the boat and taught from there. He had no need to ask Peter's permission. When Jesus finishes teaching, he directs Peter to sail to deeper water and lower the nets. Peter wonders what this landlubber from Nazareth could possibly know about fishing. They caught nothing in a night's work, but Peter decides to humor Jesus. Behold, he snags a huge catch that begins tearing the nets! Jesus did a big favor for these fishermen who were in heavy debt to Levi the toll collector who brokered their fishing rights. If Jesus could do such favors for his friends, he was indeed a friend to hang on to. When they beached the boats, "they left everything and followed him" (Luke 5:11).

Healing, a Political Activity

Then they brought to him a demoniac who was blind and mute. He cured the mute person so that he could speak and see. All the crowd was astounded, and said, "Could this perhaps be the Son of David?" But when the Pharisees heard this, they said, "This man drives out demons only by the power of Beelzebul, the prince of demons." But he knew what they were thinking and said to them, "Every kingdom divided against itself will be laid waste, and no town or house divided against itself will stand. And if Satan drives out Satan, he is divided against himself; how, then, will his kingdom stand? And if I drive out demons by Beelzebul, by whom do your own people drive them out? Therefore they will be your judges. But if it is by the Spirit of God that I drive out demons, then the kingdom of God has come upon you. How can anyone enter a strong man's house and steal his property, unless he first ties up the strong man? Then he can plunder his house. Whoever is not with me is against me, and whoever does not gather with me scatters. . . .

"When an unclean spirit goes out of a person it roams through arid regions searching for rest but finds none. Then it says, 'I will return to my home from which I came.' But upon returning, it finds it empty, swept clean, and put in order. Then it goes and brings back with itself seven other spirits more evil than itself, and they move in and dwell there; and the last condition of that person is worse than the first. Thus it will be with this evil generation" (Matt 12:22-30, 43-45).

Toward the end of Jesus' career when he entered the Temple, the chief priests and elders asked him: "By what authority are you doing these things? And who gave you this authority?" (Matt 21:23). The Greek word translated "authority" can also mean "power." Both concepts belong to the realm of politics. (Recall that kinship and politics are the only two free-standing social institutions known to our ancestors in the faith. "Religion" was embedded in both as political religion, i.e., the Temple, and domestic religion, i.e., household gods and ancestrism. So too was economics embedded in both as political economics, i.e., provisioning the Temple, and domestic economics, i.e., managing the household.)

The chief priests and elders would be the ones to grant permission or authority to teachers. But they did not authorize or empower Jesus, hence they ask this pointed question. Jesus, of course, doesn't answer their question. Actually, Jesus rarely answers questions put to him. No question is considered innocent. Every question in that culture was considered a challenge. What if the person doesn't know the answer to the question? He will be shamed. So everyone has an answer to the question, even if, as is often the case with Jesus, it is another question (or a lie).

The practice of politics has three moments: explanation, prediction, action. The candidate for public office offers his analysis and interpretation of the situation (explanation). Then he tells voters what he plans to do to remedy the situation, and how his opponent's remedy will not work (prediction). Upon election, the candidate sets his policies in motion (action). This same threefold process applies to healing: diagnosis, prognosis, therapy. Because healing deals with power, it is political in its structure and application.

Applying the model to this healing deed, a man is brought to Jesus who is possessed by a demon, is blind, and is mute (Matt 12:22, the diagnosis). Jesus heals the mute person so that he could now speak and see (Matt 12:22, the therapy). Observe the brevity of the report. The diagnosis and therapy are presented in a single verse, yet the entire episode extends for many verses.

In the Gospels, Jesus' mighty deeds (this rather than "miracle" is the correct translation of the Greek word) evoke mixed reactions. The positive reaction here wonders whether Jesus could be "the Son of David." In all the Synoptic Gospels, but especially in Matthew, Jesus' healing power is associated with this title. This association suggests that Jesus does indeed have authority and power, namely, that of the Davidic dynasty. The negative reaction from the Pharisees is a charge that Jesus is himself possessed by "Beelzebul, the prince of demons."

Westerners might say that "sticks and stones will break my bones but names will never hurt me." It is not likely anyone believes that. In antiquity, name-calling was a way of enhancing a person's honor (Son of David, prophet, teacher) or seeking to undermine or destroy it (in cahoots with Beelzebul, imbalanced, possessed by demons). This latter case is technically known in anthropology as witchcraft accusation. Witchcraft is that activity by which a person blames a personal misfortune on the aggressive activity of a member of a class of human beings (witches, wizards, and the like) who are believed to possess special power and propensity for evil. No one denied that Jesus had power. No one denied that Jesus was instrumental in healing people. The question was: where did Jesus get this power? Who gave it to him? (Matt 21:23). In this present healing episode, there are two views: Jesus has legitimate power as descendent of David, or he has evil power because of an alliance with Beelzebul.

The charge of witchcraft against Jesus by the Pharisees need not necessarily reflect their genuine opinion. It could well be a lie fabricated to discredit Jesus. In a society where honor is the paramount value, secrecy, lying, and deception are legitimate strategies to enhance one's honor and/or shame others. Still, Jesus responds once again as he does in nearly all other such hostile encounters. He levels a counter charge: "If I drive out demons by Beelzebul, by whom do your own people drive them out?" What criteria do his accusers use to distinguish exorcists gifted by God from exorcists in league with demonic forces? It is also important to note that this ability was not unique to Jesus but was familiar in his culture since other Israelites also had that power.

As he continues, Jesus manifests the typical Middle Eastern trait of speaking before thinking or even while they are thinking but still sorting out opinions. First Jesus speaks of the silliness of their charge. What would Satan benefit from driving minions out of people he surely wants to possess? And if you charge me with possession, are your relatives and others in this society similarly possessed? But, it begins to become clear to Jesus that if indeed it is by God's power that Satan is vanquished, then surely the reign of God is being established. This indeed is what life should be like when God is properly in charge.

The conclusion of this conflict is again typical. Jesus divides the world into two groups: believer versus unbeliever, good versus bad. "He who is not with me is against me!" There is no middle ground, nor is there a possibility of reconciliation.

The reader has to negotiate verses added by Matthew (which we omit here) to reach the middle element in the political/healing process: prediction/prognosis (vv. 43-45). The spirit returns to the exorcised person but, finding it difficult to repossess him, it gathers seven others to achieve their common goal. At one level this is Jesus' advice to the healed person. If you remain loyal to me, you will remain free. If you don't, your next bout will be worse than this one. At another level this parable (vv. 43-45) is directed to those who charge Jesus with witchcraft and implies that those who made the charge that Jesus is possessed are themselves possessed.

The end result of viewing Jesus' healing deeds as unauthorized political activity is that he must be stopped. "Then the chief priests and the elders of the people [the same ones who asked about his authority or power] assembled in the palace of the high priest, who was called Caiaphas, and they consulted together to arrest Jesus by treachery and put him to death" (Matt 26:3-4).

Secrecy, Deception and Lying in the Service of Honor

> Now Peter was sitting outside in the courtyard. One of the
> maids came over to him and said, "You too were with Jesus
> the Galilean." But he denied it in front of everyone, saying, "I
> do not know what you are talking about!" As he went out to
> the gate, another girl saw him and said to those who were
> there, "This man was with Jesus the Nazorean." Again he de-
> nied it with an oath, "I do not know the man!" A little later
> the bystanders came over and said to Peter, "Surely you too
> are one of them; even your speech gives you away." At that he
> began to curse and to swear, "I do not know the man." And
> immediately a cock crowed. Then Peter remembered the
> word that Jesus had spoken: "Before the cock crows you will
> deny me three times." He went out and began to weep bitterly
> (Matt 26:69-75).

When Western believers hear that in the Mediterranean
world, secrecy, deception, and lying are legitimate and acceptable strategies for defending one's honor, they often ask:
"What about the commandment?" The command they have
in mind is: "You shall not bear dishonest witness against
your neighbor" (Deut 5:20; Exod 20:16, "false witness"). Similar sentiments are expressed in Exod 23:1; Deut 19:16ff.;
Prov 19:5, 9; 24:28. The context is the court of law. In ancient Israel, this was the gathering of the elders at the city
gate. Here grievances could be settled, and presumably here
one could find justice. Yet the repeated warning against false
witnessing suggests that such witnessing may have been very
common. Was going to court such a smart idea? Indeed, a
centuries-long standing Mediterranean cultural conviction is
that going to court is an admission of failure.

It is clear that Peter is lying when he denies knowing or
being associated with Jesus. And it is quite likely that his accusers also knew for a fact that he was lying. Their goal was
to see how well Peter could lie his way out of his predicament. Peter's denial of Jesus is reported in all three of the
Synoptics (Mark 14:66-72; Luke 22:56-62) and John (18:17-
18, 25-27). Matthew has the most interesting development.
First, a woman addresses Peter directly (but loud enough for
all to hear) and claims he had been associated with Jesus.

This is a public charge, and Peter responds "in front of every one" that he has no idea what she is talking about. Recall that in this society, a woman is not a man's equal. A man can ignore any public attempt at conversation by a woman. But the charge is too dangerous for Peter to ignore, so he replies with a lie. Then another woman makes the same charge as he went out the gate. This time he denies it with an oath: "I do not know the man."

Because deception and lying are such an integral and acceptable part of this culture, a legitimate strategy for defending one's honor, how can one ever know the other is telling the truth? How can one convince a listener that he indeed is telling the truth? To accomplish this, one adds an oath. For example, in reply to Nathan's parable (2 Sam 12:1-6) about a wealthy man who took the one ewe lamb of a poor man to feed a visitor, David says: " As the Lord lives, the man who has done this merits death." To phrase it differently: "That man should die, so help me God!" The phrase Jesus repeats so often in John's gospel, "Amen, amen [or Truly, Truly], I say to you," could be paraphrased: "I'm not lying about this," or "Believe me, I am speaking the truth." Recall that Jesus did not add such an oath when he denied that he was going up to Jerusalem but later went up in secret (John 7:8, 10). But Peter is lying with an oath in direct violation of God's command: "You shall not swear by my name falsely, and so profane the name of your God: I am the Lord." God is not pleased to be summoned as a witness to someone's lie.

Finally, the bystanders say that Peter's accent betrays him (the guttural style of pronunciation peculiar to Galilee). To this third accusation, Peter swears and curses himself to bolster his denial: "I do not know the man." Ruth swore a similar oath to convince her mother-in-law, Naomi, that her promise to remain with Naomi is true and not a lie. The oath convinced Naomi of the truth of Ruth's statement (Ruth 1:17-18).

Peter's lies were definitely told to avoid trouble, to avoid getting arrested and put on trial with Jesus. In the Middle East, it is an acceptable strategy to lie to avoid trouble. From another perspective, it is also possible that Peter is lying to cover an unintended failure. After the supper on the way to the Mount of Olives, Jesus observed that all will abandon him this evening, but Peter insists: "Though all may have their faith in you shaken, mine will never be" (Matt 26:33). In reply to Jesus' statement that before the cock crows Peter will deny him three times, Peter is all the more adamant: "Even though I should have to die with you, I will not deny you" (Matt 26:35). The others agreed.

Yet just a short while later in the garden when Jesus was arrested, "all the disciples left him and fled" (Matt 26:56). Thus, when he is accused of being associated with Jesus three times (Matt 26:69-75), Peter denies Jesus in order to cover his completely unintended abandonment of Jesus in the garden. Even if none but the disciples in the story line know of Peter's loud affirmations of loyalty, the readers know he has broken his word to Jesus.

Would Jesus be upset by Peter's lies? Likely not. Jesus, too, engaged in deception to keep his opponents off balance (John 7:8, 10). Everyone did what they could to stay out of trouble, to avoid difficulties. What was more disappointing to Jesus was Peter's failed loyalty. Peter was deeply aware of this failure. Faith in the Middle East is best translated as loyalty. "I'm sticking with you no matter what." Obviously, the disciples and Peter did not stick with Jesus. When charged with this three times by outsiders, Peter lies to cover his failed loyalty as well as to stay out of trouble.

Jesus Receives Unimaginable Honor from God

After the sabbath, as the first day of the week was dawning, Mary Magdalene and the other Mary came to see the tomb. And behold, there was a great earthquake; for an angel of the Lord descended from heaven, approached, rolled back the stone, and sat upon it. His appearance was like lightning and his clothing was white as snow. The guards were shaken with fear of him and became like dead men. Then the angel said to the women in reply, "Do not be afraid! I know that you are seeking Jesus the crucified. He is not here, for he has been raised just as he said. Come and see the place where he lay. Then go quickly and tell his disciples, 'He has been raised from the dead, and he is going before you to Galilee; there you will see him.' Behold, I have told you." Then they went away quickly from the tomb, fearful yet overjoyed, and ran to announce this to his disciples. And behold, Jesus met them on their way and greeted them. They approached, embraced his feet, and did him homage. Then Jesus said to them, "Do not be afraid. Go tell my brothers to go to Galilee, and there they will see me" (Matt 28:1-10).

At the very beginning of this study while reflecting on the genealogy and origins of Jesus, we noted that Jesus died a criminal's death, a very shameful event. The man in whom so many put their trust seemed to have failed them. But gospel reports such as this one in Matthew indicate that many people saw the risen Jesus. Only God can raise someone from the dead. If God did this for Jesus, then Jesus, his life and mission, were pleasing to God. In the light of this experience, much of Jesus' life and ministry were reinterpreted, beginning with his origins, birth, and abbreviated childhood. While focusing on Matthew, let us look closer at the reports of sightings of the risen Jesus.

Here in Matthew, the Sabbath had ended and Passover observances were concluded, so the disciples may have begun making preparations to return to Galilee. Perhaps the caravan had already departed. The women arrive at the tomb and find it empty (v. 6). They also meet the risen Jesus (vv. 9-10). The women are told that Jesus "has been raised" (v. 6) and are to tell the same to Jesus' disciples (v. 7). The passive voice indicates God raised Jesus, hence God honored Jesus. The women's personal experience of the risen Jesus assures them this is real, this event actually took place.

The nature of this sighting of the risen Jesus is an altered state of consciousness experience. Ninety percent of the people on the face of this planet have such experiences routinely, since all human beings experience a variety of states of consciousness throughout the day and even during sleep. Daydreaming, road hypnosis, reverie produced by music or art are but some of the twenty different states of consciousness of which human beings are capable, including "normal, waking" consciousness!

Psychiatric research indicates that people who lose a loved one to death can and do continue to experience that loved one for many years, most commonly within the first ten years of loss. The experience and its location vary from culture to culture. In Israel, the experience is especially associated with the ancestral tomb. In modern Israel, Moroccan Jews repatriated to Israel substituted new sites and shrines for those they left behind. They make a pilgrimage to the tomb of Rabbi Simeon Bar-Yohai (second century C.E.) at Meron near Zefat on the anniversary of his death. They have substituted him for a Moroccan Holy Man. There they hold a memorial celebration followed by a picnic. Many have dreams of this Holy Man in which they experience healing, receive solutions to family problems, or other desired assistance from him.

Matthew reports that Mary Magdalene and the other Mary met Jesus at the tomb. Other gospel reports tell of appearances at the tomb, either of Jesus (John 20:14-18) or someone else (e.g., an angel): Matt 28:1-7; Mark 16:5-7; Luke 14:1-11; John 20:11-13. The risen Jesus is also met away from the tomb: Matt 28:8-10, 16-20 (in Galilee, a four- or five-day journey from Jerusalem!); Luke 24:13-35, 36-53; John 20:19-23, 24-29; John 21).

Research also indicates that there is a pattern to such experiences across cultures. First, the visionary is frightened by the experience; second, the visionary does not recognize the figure; third, the figure offers a word of calming reassurance; and fourth, the figure identifies self. Then the figure offers information sought by the visionary. All these elements need not be in every experience, but they are common in the way the experience is reported across cultures. In Matthew's report, the guards and the women are frightened by the earthquake and by the figure whose appearance is almost blindingly bright and who rolls the stone away then sits on it.

The figure doesn't identify himself to the women, but his bright appearance indicates to anyone familiar with Israelite Scripture that this figure is from the realm of God. In the Israelite tradition, light is the manifestation of God's honor or glory (Isa 60:1; 62:1; Luke 2:9), that is, God's very self. The light takes the form of a cloud (Exod 24:15ff.) or fire (Deut 5:24) flashing brightly (Ezek 1:4, 27-28; 10:4). Matthew identifies the figure as "an angel of the Lord" and the women seem to know or suspect this.

Then he offers calming reassurance: "Do not be afraid!" Finally, the angel gives information to help them with a life problem: if the tomb is empty, where is Jesus now? "He is not here, he has been raised [by God, of course!] from the dead." Then he instructs them to tell the news to the disciples and to go meet Jesus in Galilee. Notice the meeting with the risen Jesus has the same elements. The women seem to recognize Jesus, yet Jesus still must calm and assure them: "Do not be afraid!" Finally, he repeats the message of the angel: "Go tell my brothers to go to Galilee, and there they will see me."

The importance of the resurrection of Jesus and the sightings of the risen Jesus cannot be overstated. It is this central event which helps modern, especially Western, believers in their struggle to understand Middle Eastern culture and its values. The Word became flesh in a very specific culture and lived its values very well. As puzzling and sometimes repulsive as those values might seem to Westerners, God was pleased with the Mediterranean Jesus. When by all the values of that culture Jesus should have been proclaimed a failure, God raised him from the dead and forced those who accepted Jesus as Messiah to reconsider and redefine honor as Jesus sought to do in his life and ministry. That challenge is perennial in every culture.

Select Resources

Mediterranean Culture and the Bible

Malina, Bruce J. *Window on the World of Jesus: Time Travel to Ancient Judea.* Louisville, Ky.: Westminster John Knox Press, 1993.

Pilch, John J., and Bruce J. Malina, eds. *Biblical Social Values and Their Meaning: A Handbook.* Peabody, Mass.: Hendrickson, 1993.

Pilch, John J. *The Cultural Dictionary of the Bible.* Collegeville: The Liturgical Press, 1999.

Relevant Roman Catholic Church Documents (On-line)

http://clawww.lmu.edu/faculty/fjust/ChurchDocs.htm

Media

Pilch, John J. *The Cultural World of Jesus.* Audio cassette program. Canfield, Ohio: Alba House Communications, 2001.

Rohrbaugh, Richard L. *Honor and Shame: Core Values of the Biblical World.* Washington, D.C.: Biblical Archaeology Society, 2001. Video cassette program, 55 minutes.

Index of Scripture Citations

Index of Cultural Terms